organize / list women
- *personality – John Johnson*
- *spiritual gifts*

Unfreezing Moves: Following Jesus
Into the Mission Field

" I have decided to follow Jesus "

Deciders
↓
Doers
↓
Dreamers

Developers ←   Disturbers
Diagners   Discouragers
↓
Disciplers p 43

what is your first childhood memory?
what do you enjoy doing?
where has God been leading you?
List positive experiences + words +
people in your life

Search for life verse – memorize it.

List tramatic
experiences
(deaths, deficiencies
divorce
discouragements)
hurts

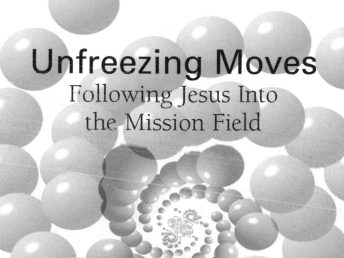

Unfreezing Moves
Following Jesus Into the Mission Field

Bill Easum

Abingdon Press
Nashville

Unfreezing Moves: Following Jesus Into the Mission Field

ISBN 0-687-05177-0

Cataloging-in-Publication data is available from the Library of Congress.

This book is printed on recycled, acid-free paper.

99 00 01 02 03 04 05 06 07 08 09 10 — 10 9 8 7 6 5 4 3 2 1
manufactured in the United States of America

Contents

Introduction
What This Book Is About

Matthew 28:18-20

This book will help congregations become more...
faithful,
permission-giving,
servant-empowering, and
constantly innovating outposts of mission,

so they can fulfill their basic reason for existence: to be with Jesus on the mission field for the purpose of making disciples who make a difference in the world.

This book isn't about church growth or church health.[1] Neither is it about how to address the various life cycles of the institutional church. Growth, health, and the life cycles of institutions are not the basic issues facing Christian congregations at the beginning of this millennium. The basic issue facing your congregation is: Are you faithful? Congregations can be healthy and growing but not faithful. Some congregations grow simply because of their location and often in spite of their best efforts to support the status quo. Many congregations, which function as a family chapel, are healthy family systems with absolutely no desire to join Jesus on the mission field. These congregations are not faithful.

I realize that some writers use the terms health and vitality somewhat in the same way I use the term faithfulness. However, too much of the writing and conversation today focuses on institutional health, which is not what I mean by the word faithfulness.

Faithful congregations follow Jesus into the mission field to make disciples who make a difference in the world. Jesus' command to "Go make disciples of all nations" (Matthew 28:19) describes the heart and soul of any authentic Christian community of faith, because it is Jesus' Last Will and Testament. Faithful congregations intentionally go out from the congregational mission post to make disciples; congregations that omit this purpose are unfaithful. No individual, congregation, or denomination is excused from this mandate, because disciple-making is the reason the Church exists. Take disciple-making away and our congregations have no justification for existence.

In the closing story to St. Luke's Gospel, as well as throughout the Acts of the Apostles, we encounter a series of "road stories." Everyone is going somewhere: Jesus on the road to Emmaus, Philip on the road to Gaza, Peter on the road to Cornelius, Paul on the road to Damascus. In these road stories, St. Luke leaves a question behind that begs to be answered: Where are all of the disciples going and why? Perhaps more importantly, where is Jesus going, and did his actions set all of this travel into motion? The answer is that they are all on the road to the Gentiles, away from the spiritual centers of religious professionals and into the world. Luke reinforces this traveling theme with the Pentecost experience, the mission of Paul to the Gentiles at Antioch, the conflict between Paul and the Jerusalem Church, and finally, Paul's mission to the West. In every instance Christianity is depicted as a movement away from the center of religious institutional, professional life into the fringes of the mission field.

Once again, God asks Christians the question: "Will you follow me again into the mission field?" If we wish to be faithful and claim the future for Jesus, we must quit trying to save our institutions and be willing to follow Jesus into the mission field, even if it means abandoning or sacrificing our institutions. The basic purpose of Christianity is to be with Jesus on the mission field. Every faithful hero in the New Testament joined Jesus on the mission field. The purpose of Christianity has nothing to do with health or growth.

Stuck and Unstuck Congregations

At the dawn of the third millennium, two kinds of churches fill the Western landscape: those that are stuck and those that are unstuck. Most Protestant congregations are stuck in the muck and mire of their institutions with little or no movement toward joining Jesus on the mission field. To them faithfulness means supporting their church and keeping it open. For them to be faithful to their God-given mission, they must be freed up from their slavery to their institutions to live for others on the mission field, freed up to function in a constantly changing world. The same can be said for denominations.

On the other hand, a growing number of congregations are joining Jesus on the mission field. They are or have become unstuck from their slavery to institutions. They are driven by a passion to connect with the outside world. Still, most of them are struggling with how to keep pace with a rapidly changing world where tried and true methodologies seldom work any longer. They are learning that in order to be faithful they must be constantly innovative in the ways they relate with those unconnected and disconnected from God.

Both stuck and unstuck congregations function the way they do because of "systems stories." A system story is the continually repeated life story or worldview of a congregation. The system story that lies buried beneath the congregation's subconscious determines the behavior of the congregation, no matter how they are organized, staffed, or programmed. Systems stories are explained in Chapter Two.

In order for stuck congregations to become faithful, they must break free of their system story and join Jesus on the mission field. To break free of this story they have to make several "unfreezing moves." In order for unstuck congregations to continue with Jesus on the mission field and develop a systems story that is innovative, they also must make a series of unfreezing moves, one on top of the other. Unfreezing moves are explained in Chapter Five.

My Purpose

My purpose for writing this book is to detail the steps for helping stuck and unstuck congregations become faithful congregations that can join Jesus on the mission, even in a rapidly changing world, because they are willing to constantly innovate. Before most congregations can be missional or innovative, they must first come to grips with the fact that they are not prepared to do either, because we live in a time when nearly everything is undergoing continual and profound transformation. To be effective in making disciples, churches must either make profound changes in the way they do ministry or constantly practice methodological innovation, neither of which is an easy task. This book is designed to help church leaders do one or the other.

My intent is not to describe why we are in this revolutionary period, or to convince people of the need for change and innovation. I leave that task to my previous books, *Dancing With Dinosaurs*, *Sacred Cows Make Gourmet Burgers*, *Growing Spiritual Redwoods*, and *Leadership on the OtherSide*. My purpose in this book is to provide a thorough, but condensed, look into how to make radical transformation or to be constantly innovative for the purpose of unleashing God's people to join Jesus on the mission field. The reader may be surprised that one book would target both needs. I can do this because the same systems story is at the heart of both long-lasting, profound transformation and the ability to constantly innovate. The key to profound change or constant innovation and improvement lies in understanding and unfreezing this systems story.

My Use of the Word Innovative

Throughout the book I will use the word innovation in a very broad sense. Some writers make a big issue out of distinguishing between innovation and adaptation.[2] I do not make that distinction in this book. Most transformations in congregations are more about adapting something being done somewhere else to fit a particular context. If the truth be known, pure innovation occurs very seldom in any discipline.

How to Use This Book

My purpose is to help congregations learn how to faithfully remain with Jesus on the rapidly changing mission field, because they constantly innovate.

This is a basic book to get you started on the road to being, or continuing to be, a permission-giving, innovative congregation. The change process I describe can be used in any size congregation. Small, medium, and large congregations are all faced with having to go through major transformations over the next few years if they want to be faithful congregations. It may surprise you to know that many of the very large, successful congregations are presently struggling with new ways to address the emerging world with the ancient Gospel.[3]

Your goal is to evaluate the condition of your congregation, and based on what you read, decide where you need to focus: whether you need to help them become unstuck or whether you need to assist your congregation in becoming or remaining innovative. The Appendix will provide you with practical references to some of the best printed resources and web sites I've discovered. A study guide for this book can be purchased at www.easumbandy.com.

Onto the Mission Field

It pains me to tell you this, but the mission field will be much different from your backyard. It will always be changing and will feel different and challenging. You will have to learn new languages and cultures. You will need to learn to be comfortable with all sorts of people and customs. You will be forced to adapt your customs and methodologies in order for your message to be received. In short, you will have to become an innovative leader in an innovative congregation.

---

1. Out of respect for my church growth colleagues, I must acknowledge that making disciples is at the heart of the work of Donald McGavran, the founder of the Church Growth Movement. Growth just has so much baggage that is becoming a hindrance to most discussions about mission today.
2. An example is Rolf Smith, *The 7 Levels of Change: Create, Innovate and Motivate With the Secrets of the World's Largest Corporations* (Arlington, TX: The Summit Publishing Group, 1997). To read about the work of Michael Kirton, who pioneered this distinction, see
   http://www.lpiper.demon.co.uk/KAIstuff/bachange.htm.
3. For more on this subject, see Donald Miller, *Reinventing American Protestantism: Christianity in the New Millennium* (Berkley: University of California Press, 1997).

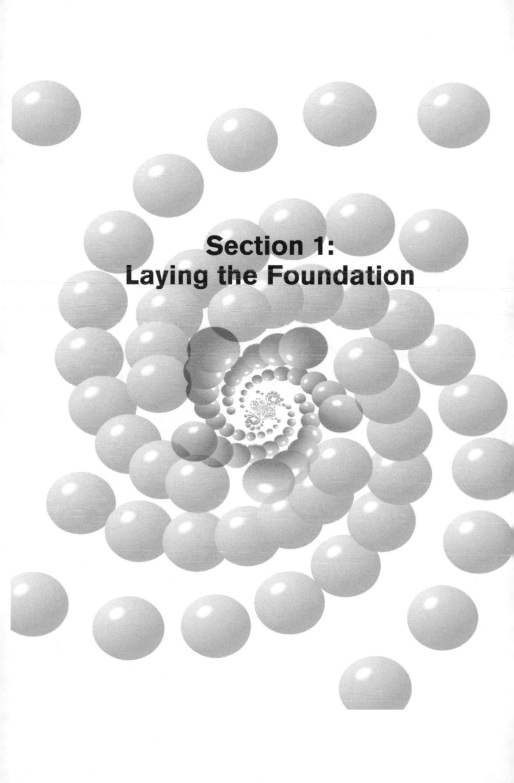

Section 1:
Laying the Foundation

Chapter 1
Christianity Is an Organic Movement

1 Corinthians 9:22

Most theories about congregational life are flawed from the start because they are based on an institutional and mechanical world-view. These views lead to the assumptions that all congregations follow a similar pattern of birth, growth, decline, and death and that their health can be fixed only for a limited amount of time. After that, they are beyond repair. Such a view is not biblical. Instead, it is fatalistic and self-serving because the goal is to fix and preserve the institution for as long a life as possible. Such a world-view allows one to focus on mere organizational and institutional survival rather than on following Jesus onto the mission field for the purpose of fulfilling the Great Commission.

However, the Old and New Testaments are based on an organic worldview. They clearly show a bias for "salvation history"[1] rather than institutional viability. Beginning with God's promise to Abraham and Sarah that they will be a blessing to all humankind, the concept of "blessed to be a blessing" has been at the heart of the Scriptures. Both Judaism and Christianity were meant to be a blessing to the rest of the world. As such, they are concerned with the movement of God throughout history, instead of the growth and health of organizations or institutions. We desperately need to recover this distinction.

Christianity is concerned with the unfolding of the Kingdom of God in this world, not the longevity of organizations. Much of the prophetic message was focused on the unfaithful leadership of those who put institutional law above bringing about change in the world. Many of the Jewish leaders of the first century were more interested in protecting the "health" or viability of their culture than pursuing the salvation history of their people. Jesus' primary criticism of these leaders was that they worshipped the institution of religion instead of the mandate to be a blessing to the world. What ultimately killed Jesus was his pursuit of this mission at the risk of self-destruction and his denial of the importance of looking after the "health" of the faith community. The same thing surfaces again in Acts 15 as the Jewish Christians are more worried about pursuing a spiritual diet plan for the community than about expanding the mission to the Gentiles.

The key to unfreezing the church to be with Jesus on the mission field is to view our congregations and denominations as the roots and shoots of an "organic movement" that go far beyond mere organizational survival. Movements are very different from institutions and behave much differently. For example, movement replaces religion, flow replaces program, midwives replace priests, mentors replace teachers, and worship is a microcosm of life's experience rather than a re-enactment of ancient history. When we understand that our congregations are part of the movement of God throughout all history, we begin to evaluate the faithfulness of our congregations based on their participation in that movement rather than factors like health or growth. We do not ask whether they are healthy or growing, but whether they are contributing to the greater movement of God in history. As such, Christianity, in whatever form it manifests itself, must never be evaluated based on institutional or mechanical standards.

Movement	Religion
A Leader	Avoids Personalities
Way of Life	Belief System
People of the Way	People of the Book
Principle	Rules
Has a Cause	Is "the Cause"
Mobile	Stationary
Common person	Elite Insiders
Servants	Entitled
Cult	Religion

To follow Jesus into the mission field means that to be effective on the mission field, Christianity must once again become a movement. As we have seen in the road stories shared by St. Luke, both his Gospel and The Acts of the Apostles portray Christianity more as a movement than a religion. It's time we recognized that fact and begin to live like disciples committed to a radical movement rather than entitled members committed to protecting our institutions.

Envisioning Christianity as a missional movement rather than an institutional model calls for restoring biblical Christianity to its role as an engager and transformer of individuals and culture rather than a fortress to protect the elitist haves (religious hierarchy) from the barbaric have-nots (pagans, Gentiles, God-fearers). It is a call to quit reducing evangelism to gaining new members and mission to sending money to denominational projects. It is a call to join Jesus on the mission field!

Movements Follow a Leader

Movements are centered around a revered leader. Remove the leader, and the movement soon becomes an institution or religion. For the first three centuries the person and work of Jesus Christ dominated the conversation. Who was he? What did he do? Why does he matter? Jesus was all that mattered. Every aspect of theology hinged on an understanding of Christology. Christianity was founded on what God did in Jesus Christ. Institutional rules, dogma, and rituals are never a substitute for a living relationship with Jesus, the leader of the Christian movement.

Imagine yourself on a mission field. You are the only Christian you know. You have spent the last several months becoming immersed in a new culture and language. Suddenly a person appears in town who claims to be a Christian. You make a straight line for that person. What is the first thing you ask that person? Do you ask the person what she or he believes, or what group she or he is aligned with? Absolutely not. You're so delighted to see another Christian that all you can do is talk about is how wonderful it is to be on the mission field with Jesus. I wish that this last sentence felt more like fact than fantasy to more of us.

Movements Embody the Spirit of the Founder

One of the earliest names for Christianity was "The Way (Acts 9:2)." Long before Christianity became known as a "faith to be believed," Christianity was a way of life that resulted from redemption in Christ. To be a Christian meant to live as Jesus lived, to join him on the mission field.

In movements that thrive long-term, subsequent leaders embody the spirit of the movement's founder. Christianity thrived because people like Paul, Apollos, Lydia, Barnabas, Peter, Mark, Stephen and others caught and lived out the resurrected spirit of Jesus by following him into the mission field. Christianity thrives today where leaders embody the spirit of Jesus. Their leadership is not based on professionalism, personality, office, or even institutional ordination. Their leadership is based on how well they emulate Jesus among the Gentiles.

Christians give their loyalty not to a set of rules or policies or a religious group, but to a person who embodied the "Way" they are supposed to live and die. This "Way" was not considered to be "one way" among many, but instead was considered to be "The Way" of all ways. As such, it demands total obedience from all disciples who claim the name Christian.

One of the problems Christianity faces today is that too much of the focus has been on the needs of the institution rather than on the task of embodying the spirit of Jesus. One example of this is the shift from being called "People of the Way" in the first century to "People of the Book" since the Reformation. Knowing the Bible often becomes a substitute for holy living. Performing rituals often replaces ethical living. The result is that faith does not automatically stimulate ethics.

Movements Are Guided by Mission Rather Than Rules

As a movement, Christianity is guided by an overriding mission, which eclipses all rules. No longer is there only one right way to do something. We now must ask what is the right thing to do in this particular part of the mission field? So how does a congregation know when to break from the established rules? It breaks when the mission is in jeopardy. Movements are fueled by a cause; institutional religion is the cause. The cause for which Christianity lives and breathes is the redemption of creation. Christians will do whatever will assist in achieving that mission.

The clash between Paul and the Jerusalem church gives us some help here. When the Jerusalem church heard that Paul had been baptizing converts without first circumcising them, they rebuked him. But after hearing of the marvelous work that was occurring in the lives of people, the council changed its mind. The guiding principle: if it transforms lives, you do it even if it is illegal because the redemption of people is more important than keeping institutional traditions. The early Christians didn't let a little thing like legality get in the way of their radical devotion to Jesus. The early Christians were fanatical about their faith, even to the point of being willing to die for their faith. That is why many considered them to be a cult.

Movements Are Mobile Rather Than Static

Movements are mobile, able to change at the whim of their leader. To be on the Way with Jesus means to be ready, willing, and able to go wherever Jesus leads us. Thus, in this time of traumatic transition, we see institutional Christianity being left behind because it is tethered to its physical moorings and can't join Jesus on the way. In its place we see the rise of House Churches, Storefront Churches, Cell Churches, Cyber Churches, Café Churches, Bar Churches, City Reaching Movements, Multiple-site churches, and Biker Churches. What do these ministries have in common? They are able to pick up and move with Jesus the moment he moves. They are not tethered to place, property, and tradition. Unfortunately, the mission field does not afford us the luxuries of stability, location, status quo, and familiarity. Nor does it allow us to try to separate reality into sacred and secular, and thus focus on "sacred space."

21

Jesus withdrew into the wilderness to pray — went to synagogue / temple to preach and proclaim.

Movements Depend on Contextual People

Large-scale movements depend on leaders who are contextual and cross-cultural. Contextual leaders are tuned in to the culture of their community. They know it like the back of their hand. They are out in the culture as much as they are in their office or spiritual community. Cross-cultural leaders are able see beyond the sacredness of any cultural form and grasp the larger mystery of what God did for all cultures. They can communicate this larger mystery in a new cultural environment. Paul's message on Mars Hill about the unknown god is an example of contextual, cross-cultural leadership. Because of his passion to share the news of Jesus, Paul was able to see beyond the cultural barrier and help the Athenians see the larger mystery. Christianity grew rapidly precisely because the message of Jesus transcended all cultural and social barriers. No one was considered untouchable. Much of present-day Christianity is too tied to one particular culture. It is time we once again opened wide the doors.

The End of Modernity's Organizational Theories

Because Christianity is a movement rather than a religion, I have a problem with the following concepts:

- Church Growth and Church Health;

- Models that describe the various sizes of congregations as family, pastoral, program, and corporate;

- The "life cycle" approach to congregational life.

These theories may well offer an accurate assessment of how mechanical, institutional organizations function, but the health and growth of congregational life have little to do with faithfully carrying out the Great Commission. Our focus should not be on congregations or denominations. It should be on how well we carry out our Lord's last request. These theories offer little or no hope if we see Christianity as an organic movement meant to encompass all existence.

Too much of what I read about "church health" and "church growth" is concerned with the survival or well-being of institutions, rather than a congregation's faithfulness to the Great Commission, which often means the self-sacrifice of individuals and groups. For example: Most congregations view the planting of a new church in close proximity to them as a threat to their survival rather than another way to enhance the Great Commission. Likewise, people with institutional worldviews have a hard time understanding the value of house churches, since they do not add members to the institutional church.

As important as the health or growth of a congregation might be to its members, it holds little importance when compared to a faithful congregation that takes seriously the Great Commission. Perhaps that is why many of our prayers for the health or survival of our congregations go unheeded. I really doubt if God cares much whether our meager institutions survive, but I do know that God cares about Christians being light, leaven, and salt to the world.

This is not to say that health and growth are unimportant. They are important. Congregations and leaders need to be healthy, and it is good if congregations grow. However, neither is directly correlated to being faithful. Faithful congregations may or may not grow, but they all give themselves away, if necessary, to fulfill the Great Commission. Faithful congregations may not be healthy, but they are faithfully making disciples of Jesus Christ. In the final analysis, all that matters is whether or not we are willing to be on the mission field with Jesus. If we are found there, we are faithful; if not, we are unfaithful.

When I wrote my first book, *The Church Growth Handbook*, published in 1990,[2] I felt the need to begin it with a biblical metaphor, which I called "the Ever-widening Circle," because I knew people would read the title from an institutional and mechanical worldview. I was a student of Donald McGavran, the founder of the Church Growth Movement, and saw how many Christian leaders dismissed him because "all he was concerned about was numbers." However, I knew that all of his work was born out of his reading of the Great Commission, especially the phrase "of all nations." His goal was never the growth of institutions. He was concerned with making disciples "of all peoples" until the day that every person of every nation could call Jesus Lord. That is what I think it means to be a faithful congregation, and that is why the health and growth of the local congregation should not be our primary focus.

A similar concern can be raised with the way some church consultants categorize congregations around terms like family, pastoral, program, and corporate, based on their size. Again, I do not wish to downplay the importance of this theory in the past. This theory works well if you have a mechanical view of organizational systems. However, in organic movements, such as the type of congregations we are seeing emerge, this theory does not work. Organic congregations seldom, if ever, begin as a family, are never pastoral or corporate; and they are much less programmatic. To be any of these is to fly in the face of an organic view of community life.

But the problem with this theory runs even deeper, and it is at this point I take exception to the theory. These categories reflect more cultural piety than biblical perspective. Family-type congregations exist for themselves, often in isolation from the environment around them and seldom, if ever, join Jesus on the mission field. Pastoral congregations require their leaders to violate some basic biblical understanding of leadership because they look to their pastor and staff for most of their ministry. (See Ephesians 4:11-12 and Acts 6.) Corporate churches seldom incorporate the concept of servanthood (humble self-giving without reward or status) among their leadership. Programmatic congregations move from one program to another, basing the faithfulness of their people on whether or not they support the programs. None of these categories can be defined as either effective on the mission field or biblically based.

The new breed of congregation emerging at the beginning of this millennium begins as a movement with a mission beyond itself. The goal of these congregations is to join Jesus on the mission field to bring about change in an area of town, in the city, and in the world. They explode and hive off into other congregations. House churches emerge here and there with little or no organizational life of their own. They mutate and proliferate into other house churches. In the traditional sense, these new congregations birth new congregations in rabbit-like fashion, giving little thought to their own institutional preservation. Movements do not have the same organizational flow as institutions. Again, these may be accurate descriptions of how congregations function today, but they should not be understood as the way faithful congregations function.

According to the proponents of "organizational life cycles," organizations have predictable life cycles that run the gamut from birth, to infancy, to expansion, to adolescence, and finally to what Ichak Adizes calls "prime."[3] From there on, the life cycle inevitably begins to deteriorate into stability, then aristocracy, then recrimination, then bureaucracy, and finally death. Although the patterns of congregational and denominational life over the past two hundred years support this theory, the past two hundred years have been based on a worldview that is mechanical, bureaucratic, and hierarchical and coupled with slow and evolutionary change.

NOTE
X

However, our worldview today is so organic and revolutionary that change is now built into the fabric of life. As a result, effective congregations think like movements, not organizations or institutions. Achieving a mission beyond the local organization is the driving principle, not some rule book or policy manual or even the survival of the institution. Organizational and institutional survival or health of the congregation is not what is at stake with movements. Rather, what is at stake is the expansion of the movement, which in this case is the fulfillment of the Great Commission. Many of the church leaders who are comfortable in institutional settings do not take the Great Commission as literally binding on them. However, the church leaders I'm seeing emerge in the organic congregations actually believe that the Great Commission could be fulfilled in their lifetime. Much is at stake on this point.

Effective leaders of movements do not seek answers to the questions, "What's wrong with our institutions?" or "How do we repair the institution?" Instead, they ask, "Why isn't the greater mission being accomplished, and what needs to happen to cause the movement to gain momentum?" The focus of faithful and innovative congregations is on the Great Commission, not the congregation or denomination.

In a way, gaining momentum is one of the keys of movements. The more momentum there is, the more expansion there will be, and the best way to continue the momentum is to never refreeze the change process. In times like these, change for the sake of change becomes a goal, so that innovation, rather than upholding the status quo, is a badge of honor that leaders proudly wear.

values of personality

innovative vs stability

When we think of our congregations as organisms rather than organizations, we soon see that the life-cycle approach no longer has any meaning. Organisms can hive, reproduce, and be grafted and transplanted, thus giving them a life far beyond that of a located, static institution. We can then see that we can no longer concern ourselves mainly with institutional survival. Now we must ask the bigger question: Have we become faithful enough to join Jesus on the mission field? Venturing forth onto the mission field may well mean abandoning our congregations or planting new ones, but it will never mean ensuring their survival. We have the assurance that the gates of hell cannot prevail against God's church. So why should we worry?

excitement of the new vs relief in expected routine

My reason for saying the life-cycle approach is flawed is not so much to criticize the theory, as to show that the theory is not helpful to a salvation history that goes far beyond congregational life. Congregational life is not our concern. The fulfillment of the Great Commission is our goal. Most church leaders are so focused on the well-being of their own congregations that they equate local church growth with Kingdom growth. We must not make that mistake. I also don't appreciate the fatalistic approach of life-cycle theory because though our fulfillment of the Great Commission may ebb and flow, it will never end.

So in a sense, all past organizational theory is going the way of the wind. Still, the reader should in no way see this analysis as a negative critique of any of the above theories. Just the opposite. They do provide an accurate analysis of how institutionally based organizations worked in the past and still hold some promise to help stuck congregations that want to survive a bit longer. But these theories hold little promise for helping congregations faithfully join Jesus on the mission field, and they won't prove useful for congregations seeking to be innovative. As we will learn in Chapter Four, innovative congregations are already proving to live by a different set of criteria.

The Measure of a Faithful Congregation

So, how do we ultimately measure the faithfulness of a congregation? Not by how well it supports the denomination, or how long it can survive, or how many new members it receives, or whether it is healthy, or even how harmonious it is. Rather we gauge faithfulness by a congregation's willingness to follow Jesus into the mission field.

Using this measure of faithfulness, congregations do one of three things when they are no longer able to connect with the unreached. They

- Begin radically new ministry based on research from the public;

- Relocate;

- Send out all of their people to various parts of the city or world to plant new mission outposts.

It is conceivable that following Jesus into the mission field could actually cause a congregation to close its doors as it births many new outposts on the mission field. The difference here from the life-cycle approach to organizations is that the institution does not matter, so its death is not the end of the movement. The movement goes on as the remaining people of the congregation spread out into new congregational outposts.

In essence this creates a "Mission Life Cycle" and offers hope and expectation, instead of the inevitable doom of the life-cycle approach. The mission life cycle points us away from our self-serving institutions and out into the mission field to be among the Gentiles, Samaritans, and God-fearers. The mission life cycle places our institutions right where they belong: in submission to the Great Commission.

Where Do We Go From Here?

We're not living in the second Reformation. We're living in the first century all over again. God is calling Christianity out of its institutional prison, out from behind the cloistered walls of the sanctuary, out from the safety of denominational dominance, out from the marriage of Church and State, away from the merger of culture and piety, away from the professionals, into the dangerous, uncontrollable, deadly byways and highways. Jesus is calling us to the back roads of real life, where once again Christians associate with pagans, Gentiles, and God-fearers. It's time to join Jesus on the mission field. Go get your traveling shoes.

---

1. For more information see
   http://www.newcreation.org.au/lib/127/html/127_01.htm.
2. Easum, William, *The Church Growth Handbook* (Nashville: Abingdon, 1990).
3. Ichak Adizes, *The Pursuit of Prime: Maximize Your Company's Success with the Adizes Program* (Santa Monica: The Knowledge Exchange, 1997).

Chapter 2
The Systems Story

Following Jesus into the mission field is either impossible or extremely difficult for the vast majority of congregations in the Western world because of one thing: They have a systems story that will not allow them to take the first step out of the institution into the mission field, even though the mission field is just outside the door of the congregation.

Every organization is built upon an underlying system, called a systems story. This is not a belief system; it is the continually repeated life story that determines how an organization thinks and thus acts. This systems story determines the way an organization behaves, no matter how the organizational chart is drawn. Restructure the organization and leave the systems story in place, and nothing changes within the organization. It's futile trying to revitalize an organization without changing the system. Your ability to discover your congregation's story is one of the keys to change and constant innovation.

Two systems stories seem to dominate stuck and unstuck congregations. Stuck congregations have a "Command-and-control, Stifling Story." Unstuck congregations have a "Permission-giving, Innovation Story." These two systems stories are at opposite poles, with many variations on the story in between. The more stuck a congregation is, the more controlling and stifling it is. The more unstuck a congregation becomes, the more permission-giving and innovative it is.

The Top-down, Command-and-control, Stifling Story

For most of the past five hundred years, the Command-and-control, Stifling Story, has shaped organizations. At its best, this system can be deemed efficient; at its worst, it can be deemed tyrannical. At the heart of this systems story is the desire to control everything that happens throughout a congregation, including individual behavior and the development of new ministries. In this system, procedure and playing by the rules are more important than the mission. Here's how this story is played out.

A person with enthusiasm brings a new ministry idea to the pastor. The pastor takes the new idea to the official body or to a few key leaders. They reject the new idea 95 percent of the time because, "We've never done that before." The pastor tells the person it can't be done. The person is disappointed and decides this is a place that does not like new ideas, and in time drops out to look for another congregation. The leaders are glad they did not respond favorably to this person's idea since the person was so uncommitted to the congregation that the person left. Over a period of years, this story is repeated again and again until the day comes when the congregational leaders are never presented with any new ideas. In this story the role of leaders is little more than the exercise of control over the spending of money or the accomplishing of anything that does not fit the opinions and culture of those who have control over the congregation.

The Bottom-Up, Out-of-control, Permission-giving, Innovation Story

A new understanding of organization is emerging, born out of quantum physics, chaos theory, and a return to biblical principles of organization. This new understanding can best be described as a Permission-giving, Innovative Story. At its best, this system spawns enormous health and personal and corporate growth; at its worst, it allows the system to run amuck. At the heart of this system is a clear direction and a high level of trust and commitment from the leaders to the consensus mission of the congregation. Here's how this system is played out.

The congregation has a clear sense of its mission or purpose in life, and has an atmosphere about it that encourages everyone to find his or her purpose. As they discover their purpose in life, they are encouraged to live out that purpose on behalf of the Body of Christ. *not on behalf of CCH* Someone brings a new idea to anyone who is currently leading a ministry that involves two or more other people. The leader examines the new idea in light of the congregation's mission. The idea does not need to go to a centralized authority for approval. If the new ministry enhances the congregation's mission, the person is given permission on the spot to put the new idea into action, if he can find two or three other people who want to do it with him. Others see how this system works and are encouraged to seek their own purpose in life. New ministries continually emerge and innovation fills the congregational life. In time, people begin to expect innovation and are worried when new ideas don't regularly emerge. The role of leadership in this story is to provide an atmosphere of trust and per mission so people can follow God's leading rather than the will of a handful of people who try to control everything that happens.

The Biblical Problem With Control

The Scriptures are full of examples of our drive to control our lives and the lives of others. The Garden of Eden, the Tower of Babel, Israel's reinterpretation of her election, the desire of the disciples to share Christ's throne, or the disciples' desire to know the time when the Kingdom would be restored, are all examples of our desire to reduce God to a manageable level. And the Bible looked upon this desire for control as sin.

Just as we desire to reduce God to a level where we can exercise enough control, our desire for control carries over into the many forms of abusive relationships within most congregations, as well as the multiple levels of management controls, checks, and balances. The mantra becomes, "Machines, institutions, decisions, and people must be kept under control!" The desire for control is so strong that no matter how far a congregation may go in innovation, given the opportunity, the systems story will revert back to Command and Control. The bottom line is that the desire of many church leaders to have control over their congregation is a form of sin. They want to play God.

This reduction of Christianity to a manageable level has resulted in mission where the dominant concern is taking care of entitled members and balancing budgets. If you doubt what I've just said, just watch how the vast majority of congregational and denominational leaders spend their time.

The problem with the present form of institutional religion is that for the most part it has reduced the Gospel to a manageable number of programs, structures, budgets, and, of course, the outcome is institutional survival. The arbitrary whims and personal opinions of a few people replace the Gospel command to equip and live out the divine gifts that are endowed each Christian. After all, committees and staff can be managed and controlled, but the gifts of the Spirit can't be kept under one's thumb.

If you think I'm being too negative, you simply have misjudged the seriousness of the subject. Control is far more than just an organizational issue. It's a tyrannical form of reducing Christianity to serve a handful of members of the institution, rather than freeing everyone up to follow the still, small voice of the ever-changing flow of the Holy Spirit. It flies in the face of what God intended for the Christian community.[1] God made us to follow the flow of the Spirit, not to be controlled by a handful of people who want to impose their personal opinions on the community. It's time we ended Christendom's captivity of God's people and set them free.[2]

How Congregations Move From Stuck to Unstuck and Constantly Innovate

The process of moving from stuck to unstuck, as well as the ability to constantly innovate, is depicted in the six graphics below. The graphics depict four different spheres of congregational life. Figure One illustrates the basic questions that are being asked in each sphere. Determining which sphere dominates the life of a congregation and how many individuals are in each sphere helps move a congregation forward. It's very normal for a congregation to be dominated by one sphere while many or most of its people are in a different sphere. It is also normal for parts of a congregation to be in one sphere while other parts are in another. The process of moving from one sphere to another is usually incrementally messy and is not a neat linear process. I've never seen a congregation in which everyone or every part is in the same sphere; but every congregation I've worked in has one dominant feeling, atmosphere, or environment that permeates everything and everyone.

Each sphere is the result of the attitude of the people in power, not the congregation. When a congregation moves from one sphere to another, it is because a person or group in power assumes a different attitude or a group with a different attitude comes into leadership. When a congregation moves from one sphere to another, the attitude of the previous sphere remains dormant for several years and can resurface without much difficulty for decades. For years, the old attitude can and usually does move into any vacuum caused by the absence of positive, forward-looking leadership. A desire for control and dislike of change is embedded deep into the human condition. As such, these characteristics are two of the main symptoms of institutional religion, which opposes Christianity as a dynamic movement.

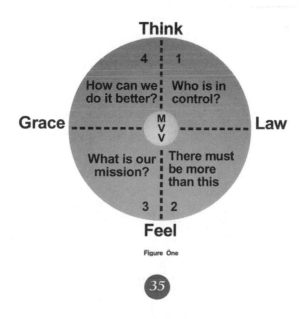

Figure One

Sphere One

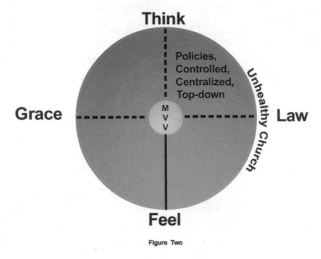

Figure Two

Congregations or individuals in Sphere One are ruled by a handful of people at the top, who are called the "Deciders." The Deciders are those who inform the congregation what ministries will or won't be accomplished in the life of the congregation. The Deciders go in search of "Doers" to carry out these ministries. "Doers" are found in the pews. These congregations rely primarily on top-down, centralized, controlling policies. Contentment, complacency, and/or fear override decisions that require a leap of faith from the leaders. Any new idea has to get the approval of the Deciders before it can become a reality. In the most severe cases, even new members have to be approved by the Deciders.

Lack of experience + inflated ego

Tightly controlled congregations do not grow people or welcome new ideas.

The problem is that passivity and despair sap the life and energy from the remaining Doers so that it becomes harder and harder to find Doers to carry out the institutional functions of the congregation. On the other hand, the feelings of the Deciders are often characterized by nostalgia. They long for the glory days of the past. Worse yet, they actually think that it is possible to return to the good old days.

Sphere One: Set your own agenda.

Congregations in this sphere are almost always stagnant, dying, and/or dysfunctional. Determining who is in control is the dominating passion. To become unstuck, congregations must move out of Sphere One. Doing so usually raises the wrath of the Deciders who often become "Controllers." As Controllers, their number-one task is to insure that change cannot occur. Innovation is impossible in a Sphere One congregation.

This kind of leadership insures two results: people are discouraged from growing spiritually or reaching their God-given potential, and new ideas are seldom welcome. In such a climate, innovation is next to impossible.

If your congregation is locked into Sphere One and you wish to transform it, your first priority is to clarify what is the non-negotiable part of your call and Jesus mission.[3] If you don't know, the Deciders/Controllers and unhealthy members will tell you. To move out of Sphere One into Sphere Three, leaders must focus on the goal of transformation, not the confusion, the fear, and the distractions of the naysayers.

Some key questions to ask yourself:

Key Q

• Am I clear about what God has called me to do?

• Is my calling clear enough that I can communicate it to others in such a way that it stimulates a response?

• Is my call worth suffering for?

• How passionate am I about transforming this congregation?

Sphere Two

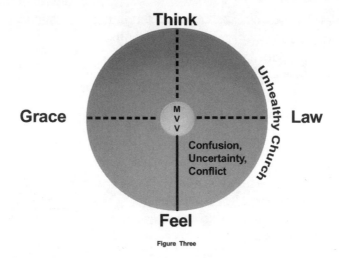

Figure Three

The feeling that "there must be more to church than this" is the dominant passion of Sphere Two. Some of the Doers, who are often not elected officials, intuitively know that something isn't right. In the past, the Doers did what the Deciders asked them to do out of a sense of duty to the institution. However, as this sense of duty erodes, as it has the past four decades, the Doers may morph into "Dreamers" who yearn for something more than they are presently getting from their congregational life. They begin to ask questions and refuse to serve dutifully on committees, and then the Deciders become unhappy Controllers.

It is always painful and messy when stuck congregations come out of Sphere One. As soon as someone begins voicing the concern that "surely there is more to life than this," the Controllers attempt to clamp down. If the Dreamers try to move the congregation into Sphere Two, confusion always occurs, and the Controllers say, "See, we told you it wouldn't work." The closer the congregation moves to Sphere Three, the more confusion, discontent, and conflict will emerge. Unfortunately, the Deciders and Controllers are usually victorious, and the Dreamers leave the congregation or become inactive. If this story is reenacted enough times, most, if not all, of the healthy dreamers leave for greener pastures. In time, the system returns to the humdrum of the Top-down, Command-and-control, Stifling Story. All is at peace, but the church continues to lose spirit and people.

If your congregation is breaking out of Sphere One into Sphere Two, leaders must focus on fanning the flames of the discontented who know that there must be more to faith than what they are receiving from their church. It has long been known that the amount of change leaders will tolerate is in direct proportion to the amount of their discontent. So more change is possible by fanning the discontented and mentoring them into a new understanding of mission. Your goal is to turn discontented people into passionate Dreamers who can envision a more authentic way of living out the mission of Jesus. Of course, you also make it more likely that the Deciders will become Controllers, and this might cause you to be in a real pickle.

Sphere Two: Fan and grow the discontented into passionate dreamers who upset the balance of the status quo.

Spend as much time as possible mentoring the potential Dreamers. Meet with them weekly. Grow them into spiritual leaders and servants who, when the time is right, can assume leadership in the church and catapult it into Sphere Three. Often, these folks will have to replace the Deciders, especially if they have become Controllers who refuse to change.[4]

This is the sphere where most would-be change agents buckle under the pressure, and the congregation slips quietly back into Sphere One, the Dreamers become victims of nightmares, and the Controllers are even more entrenched than before. If you plan on starting the push to Sphere Three, don't buckle under the pressure—and there will be pressure. Don't make the mistake of thinking that the controllers are not organized to remain in control. Such a mistake can be fatal.

For example, the pastor may be frustrated in attempts to start a second, more informal worship service. A group of Dreamers emerges among the grass roots and begins meeting in homes to plan an alternative format for worship. But the half-time adult choir director, who is technically competent, has thwarted such attempts in the past and is not the spiritual leader required for a more participatory format of worship. The discontented Dreamers capture the imagination of the church board, and there appears to be the will to move forward by redesigning the music ministry and seeking a more spiritual music director to guide the core worship ministries in the church. But the personnel committee of the board is stacked with loyal choir members who caucus and protect the job of the adult choir director and demand a search for a new pastor.

Sphere Three

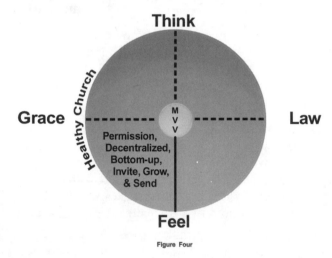

Figure Four

To move into Sphere Three, the leaders and newly emerging Dreamers must continually fan the discontentment among the Doers without causing them to lose their courage. Such courage does not come easy in the face of staunch, long-term Controllers. Developing or recovering a passion for making disciples and changing leadership are the keys to moving through this sphere.

Often, before fully entering Sphere Three, all-out war breaks out. It is not unusual for a congregation to lose ten to twenty percent of its membership while moving from Sphere One to Sphere Three. If and when Controllers decide to leave, let them. Perhaps they will find a suitable church somewhere else. The sad truth is that many of them will assist in the ruin of another congregation.

Be warned: It's one thing to transform a congregation from Sphere One to Sphere Three if it is healthy and isn't full of Controllers; it is another to try to move it when it is either full of Controllers or totally dysfunctional. So, if you are in a church that is deep into the worst part of Sphere One as it can get, decide early on if you have what it takes to begin the transformation. It is one thing to "dance with dinosaurs,"[5] it is another to be up to your neck with "raptors."

By now you also realize that unfreezing a stuck congregation or keeping a congregation constantly innovating is not a slam-dunk. Even though you are successful, you know that for years, given the chance, the system can revert to what it was. So here are a few pointers to keep in mind if you see the system reverting to the old status quo.

- If resistance runs high, don't blink. Instead, bolster your personal resolve and remember why you began the process. The worst thing you can do is bail out on the troops.

- Rev up the amount of resources you are funneling to your leaders and spend more time encouraging those who are in the Dreamer stage.

- Teach your leaders not to listen to those who are constantly complaining. All that does is encourage the self-centered complainers.

- Continually replenish your leadership base so that people on the front line of the conflict or people who have been at the forefront of innovation can take a breather and personally enter into Sphere Four for personal renewal.

- Build in spiritual renewal retreats for your leadership. Both conflicts and innovation can be draining.

• If staying up with constant innovation is getting to you, then build in regular times each quarter where you can get away and spend some time either alone or with leaders a step ahead of you.

Sphere Three: Organize to identify, recruit, equip, deploy, and coach those who are ready.

Every stuck congregation that moves out of Sphere One to Sphere Three always seems to go through the confusion found in Sphere Two. Just about everyone I talk with confesses that initially the shift from command-and-control to permission-giving is confusing because "we've never done it that way before." Spiritually mature people ask questions that they would ask only if they had been in a command-and-control system all of their lives. So tell your leaders that a period of confusion on their part is normal and that it is okay to have many questions. Trust the system to work, and new ways of accomplishing ministry will surface in time. The confusion and discomfort will pass as much more ministry begins to bubble up from the grass roots. Also, don't be surprised or dismayed if confusion is still present in the early months or years of Sphere Three.

Figuring out "Why are we here," or how does this enhance our mission?" is the dominant passion of Sphere Three. Congregations or individuals in this sphere function better around freedom, trust, permission-giving, and servant empowerment. Innovation and mistakes commonly occur together. Mistakes should be seen as a second chance to get it right. People learn from the mistakes and growth occurs. These congregations are shaped by a chaotic uncertainty that fuels a nuclear-like chain reaction of growth. Synergy is birthed like crazy in the Sphere Three congregation. Excitement runs high. People invite their neighbors to worship with them, and new leaders regularly emerge. People are empowered. New ministries bubble up in every cell and at every level of the congregation.

Congregations that are constantly innovating usually move in and out of Sphere Three and Four. It is unusual for an organization to sustain rapid growth and remain in Sphere Three for decades. However, when it does, there need to be three crucial things: more common sense; more time away for the key leaders to experience other innovative congregations; and a much more intentional and systematic approach to growth and health.

If your congregation has moved into Sphere Three, the goal of your leaders is to identify, recruit, equip, deploy, and coach those who are ready to become apprentices and leaders. Systems are developed that assist this goal. A loving, caring, and accepting community of leaders who base their life together on trust rather than control begins to grow. The more the community grows in its trust of one another, the easier it is for new converts and seekers to see faith in action. We will see the importance of a community of trust in the next chapter.

Sphere Four

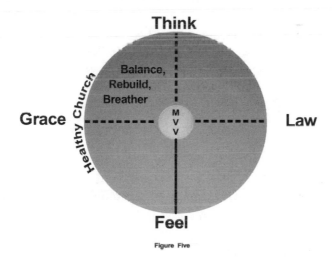

Figure Five

Sphere Three congregations move into Sphere Four when they need a breather from the rapid growth. The dominant passion of this sphere is discovering how to do things better. Improvement is more important at this sphere than innovation, which is often put on hold for the moment. This sphere can be little more than time to take a breather from innovation, or it can be as serious as regrouping and retraining the leadership. Key questions are: What do we do next? Who will be our new leaders? What do we have to do to rebuild? Is it time to return to Sphere Three and resume growth and innovation? However, as soon as the congregation has had time to regroup and train or retrain its leaders, the leadership needs to re-ignite the congregation by returning to Sphere Three.

Think of Sphere Four as troops in battle taking a fallback position so that they can regroup to fight another day. Congregations enter Sphere Four so they have time to rekindle the passion for the Mission, Vision, and Values (DNA); discover new leaders; train and retrain the leadership; and above all, avoid a long, slow, slump into Sphere One. Just as troops on the battlefield do not remain in retreat, the fallback position is understood to be temporary. The eventual goal of falling back is to move forward. So complacency and contentment are the key enemies to guard against in Sphere Four. To remain in Sphere Four too long is the same as returning to Sphere One, thus changing system stories throughout the congregation. Congregations need to move into Sphere Four and take a breather when one or more of the following begins to happen:

Sphere Four: Time to take a breather and regroup.

- Leaders become overly tired and unimaginative;

- New leaders become hard to find;

- The growth is outstripping the congregation's ability to equip leaders and adequately respond to the influx of people; or

- Rapid growth is beginning to degrade the quality of congregational life.

I had a conversation with one of the leading pastors in North America that demonstrates the importance of moving in and out of Spheres Three and Four in thriving congregations. This congregation has a goal of planting hundreds of congregations over the next twenty years. At the time of conversation, they had planted approximately twenty congregations. The pastor said to me, "Bill, we are putting new congregation plants on hold for the moment. We are running short of trained leaders for starting all of these congregations. (The congregation has sent out several hundred people with each new start.) When we develop enough new leaders, we will return to our passion to plant congregations." This congregation had just moved into Sphere Four. A few months later, they returned to Sphere Three and resumed their planting efforts.

Most congregations that are constantly innovating move in and out of Sphere Three and Sphere Four, ensuring balanced, long-term growth and stability. Sphere Three is the place for leaders to go when things become normal, dull, and the status quo begins to be savored. Sphere Four is the place to go when things become too hectic.

The Innovative Church

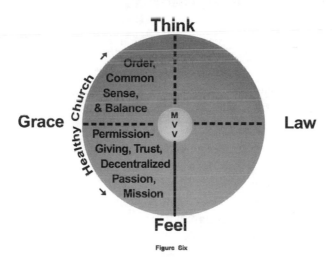

Figure Six

The key to becoming unstuck or being constantly innovative is learning how to move in and out of Sphere Three and Four. To do this, Christian leaders must rely more on:

- Scripture than church policies
- Holy Spirit than charters, constitutions, policies, or denominational manuals
- Transformed leaders than restructured organizations
- A leader's passion than job descriptions
- Trust than control

- The power of grass roots than centralized authority
- "We ought to try this since we've never done it" than "we've never done it that way before and we aren't going to start now"
- Teams than committees
- Called and equipped people than plans or programs
- Transformed than informed lives
- Embodied faith than a memorized faith
- Building strong character than consensus.

Before Reading Further

Before reading further, write down the sphere that best describes the actions of your leadership and then the sphere in which you find most of the congregation. The leadership of my congregation acts as if they are in Sphere _____on its way to Sphere_____. Most of the congregation appears to be in Sphere _____.

Keep in mind that a relationship exists between the speed of transformation and the sphere in which the critical mass of the people reside. If the leaders are in Sphere One and most of the congregation is in Sphere Two, a leader can be more aggressive. If both the leaders and most of the congregation are in Sphere One, the transformation will be more difficult and take much longer because of the amount of opposition to change and the lack of people who are discontented with the condition of the congregation.

---

1. See Acts 14-16.
2. Christendom is that period of time from AD 361, when Constantine made Christianity the official religion of the Empire, until the present day. For a brief, but thorough, description of Christendom, see Bill Easum, *Leadership on the OtherSide* (Nashville: Abingdon Press, 2000).
3. For more on the importance of the call to transformation, see Bill Easum, *Leadership on the OtherSide* (Nashville: Abingdon Press, 2000).
4. Michael Slaughter, pastor of Ginghamsburg UMC, (www.ginghamsburg.org) often tells the story of how he spent the first year of his tenure training a group of new leaders and then replacing the old leaders with them. My experience at the church I served for twenty-four years was much the same.
5. William M. Easum, *Dancing With Dinosaurs* (Nashville: Abingdon Press, 1993).

Chapter 3
Permission-giving Communities of Faith

Trusting the Spirit to run wild through the congregation, instead of relying on rules and policies, is a key ingredient of faithful and innovative congregations.

Churches stuck in Sphere One never join Jesus on the mission field. On the mission field, the number-one challenge facing Christian congregations today is learning how to develop permission-giving, servant-empowering, innovative environments that trust the Spirit to run wild through the congregation.

A Crash Course on Permission Giving

The following is a crash course on the permission-giving congregation. For a complete account, see my book *Sacred Cows Make Gourmet Burgers*.[1] A permission-giving, servant-empowering congregation is a community where persons are encouraged to discover and live out their God-given gifts:

• in order to enhance the agreed-upon mission of the church;

• without having to ask for permission from a central authority; and

• as long as they can find two or three people who want to help and what they do does not violate the DNA.

The result: innovation bubbles up everywhere. Three things form the core of permission-giving congregations. In the essentials, they require unity of purpose. Being clear on which values are non-negotiable is at the heart of the permission-giving congregation. In the nonessentials, they provide freedom and empowerment to innovate. The primary role of all leaders is to equip others for ministry. In all things, they expect love, respect, and collaboration.

The goals of thriving, permission-giving, servant-empowering, innovative congregations are:

- To transform lives through a personal relationship with Jesus Christ;

- To provide a safe and loving place where those who are unconnected to Jesus can experience the difference he can make in their lives;

- To provide an environment in which people are encouraged and empowered to discover and use their God-given gift and talent for the advancement of the kingdom;

- To grow spiritual giants who grow other spiritual giants;

- To embrace new ministries that enhance the congregational DNA;

- To justify before the congregation any negative decision;

- To reduce voting to a bare minimum, and to employ prayer and discernment in its place;

- To initiate most new ministries among the grass roots;

- To have most decisions made on the spot, any time, by any leader;

- To decide on major issues in less than sixty days;

- To enhance the consensus DNA of the church (Mission, Vision, and Values);

- To do all the administrative work by a small Leadership Team that supports and equips the ministry teams;

- To pump the information flow in and out of the Leadership Team on a regular basis;

- To celebrate that every person in the congregation is a minister with a ministry;

- To organize the congregation around the DNA.

Two behavioral changes must happen for permission-giving systems to flourish: Paid servants must give up control of ministry and begin equipping others for ministry; unpaid servants (formerly laity or volunteers) must give up control of the administration and begin to do most, if not all, of the pastoral ministry. These behavioral changes are the reason transformation is so difficult. It goes to the heart of how people have behaved for decades.

The Role Of Permission-giving, Servant-Empowering Leaders

Every faithful congregation needs a leader of leaders who is surrounded by well-equipped leaders whose goal it is to say yes to anything that enhances the consensus mission of the church.

To promote permission giving these leaders should:

• Provide an environment where people are encouraged to grow spiritually, to discover their God-given gifts, and to put those gifts into motion. This environment is set by the leaders, who say yes to all new ideas, as long as they do not violate the DNA.

• See in the other members of the congregation what God sees in them, help them discover their gifts, and then get out of their way. To accomplish this, leaders must be good listeners and concentrate on relationships more than on personal accomplishment.

• Insure that each person is discipled before they are placed into leadership.

• Stand up to the Controllers by not allowing them to set the environment and asking them to leave if necessary.

• Be flexible on most things, but extremely clear on the DNA.

• Be comfortable being out-of-control and with making mistakes.

• Demonstrate that fulfilling the mission is more important than how it is fulfilled.

The following practical steps have helped many leaders become more permission-giving as well as begin the process of destabilizing a system.

- Moving toward permission giving usually begins with the pastor simply giving people permission to experiment with ministry without getting any official form of approval. The pastor says something like "Just try it and see how it works. See how many other people are interested in it, then go for it. When you get a little success under your belt, we'll go to the board and let them see how it has changed lives and enhanced the congregation." Many of these new ministries will do very well, which can give Dreamers encouragement and help lower the fear level among the Deciders. In congregations where the DNA has not been established, often these new ministries help Deciders see that the roof did not cave in when these people deployed their ministry without approval from a centralized authority. In the early going of transformation, when Controllers challenge such action, the pastor can always ask for forgiveness—it is easier to obtain than permission. It is also easier for pastors to ask for forgiveness in their first year as pastor of a church. Perhaps that's the reason that over 95% of all successful turnarounds I've seen began in the first year of pastor's tenure.

- Avoid taking a vote on new ministries whenever possible. When confronted by Controllers, remind them that the early church prayed for guidance rather than voting. It is amazing how disarming and powerful it is when a leader says, "Lets spend an hour praying about this and listening to what God has to say before we vote."

- Let out-of-date programs or committees die with dignity instead of trying to prop them up.

- Make up an excuse not to attend meetings where you know nothing is going to happen. Make a list of committees that your church wouldn't miss if they didn't exist, those that are causing harm to your church, and those that are absolutely necessary to your church and schedule your time accordingly.

- As often as you can, give new ideas to newly appointed teams instead of standing committees.

- In the early going of moving towards destabilizing a system and/or moving toward permission giving, the leaders should test their readiness for permission giving and determine where the bumps and detours might be moving from Sphere One to Sphere Three. A good way to determine readiness is for the Dreamers to fill out the permission-giving inventory in Appendix A. Do one inventory based on how the Dreamers feel about their own readiness and one on how they feel about the Deciders/Controllers' readiness. Then compare the two. Your answers to the questions will give you some guidance about what you still need to learn as well as what you feel more comfortable with.

• Spend the necessary time laying a foundation for permission-giving by reacquainting your Dreamers with the Scriptures and by pointing them toward as many spiritual formation types of experiences as possible.[2]

For more on permission giving, see my book *Sacred Cows Make Gourmet Burgers*, pages 71-95 and our video resource "Sacred Cows Make Gourmet Burgers" at www.easumbandy.com. For a sample list of permission-giving congregations, see http://www.easumbandy.com/FAQS/permissiongivingchurches.htm.

---

1. William M. Easum, *Sacred Cows Make Gourmet Burgers* (Nashville: Abingdon Press, 2000).
2. The following texts will help you ground your leaders for transformation: John 21:16; Matthew 28:18-20; Ephesians 4:11-12; Acts 10 and 17; 1 Corinthians 9:22; 1 Peter 5:2-4; Romans 12:6-21; Isaiah 43:19.

Chapter 4 The Innovative Congregation

The permission-giving organization is by nature an innovative environment that is constantly keeping the status quo from forming (homeostasis). Any time new ministries are allowed to bubble up from the grass roots, without the approval of a centralized authority, innovation is inevitable. However, it is one thing to be unintentionally innovative. It is quite another thing to be intentionally innovative. To be intentional does not mean that innovation can be planned or programmed. It means that innovation is encouraged and nurtured.

Innovative congregations revolve around and receive their passion from their DNA. Tom Bandy and I refer to DNA as purpose, that is, the agreed-upon Mission, Vision, Values, and Bedrock Beliefs of the congregation.[1] Everything a congregation does—every decision, every dollar spent, every person hired or terminated—is based on whether or not the action will enhance the DNA.

Innovative Leaders

Innovative congregations are led by leaders who have a passion for being on the mission field with Jesus. I've learned from personal experience and from observing other leaders that the ability to innovate results more from a passion for mission than from a skill one possesses. Christian innovators so desperately want to communicate God that when the mission is no longer being achieved, they experiment until new ways are found to achieve the mission. Because of this rabid commitment to the mission, innovative leaders will try almost anything, even if it violates their denomination or congregational polity, as long as it does not violate their DNA and promises to enhance the mission.

As a result, these leaders become what I call "contextual innovators." Contextual innovators are tuned in to the culture of their community. They know it like the back of their hand. They are out in the culture as much as they are in their office or among their congregation. Contextual are able see beyond the sacredness of any cultural form and he larger mystery of what God did for all cultures. They can communicate this larger mystery in a new cultural environment. Paul's message on Mars Hills about the unknown god is an example of contextual, cross-cultural leadership. Because of his passion to share the news of Jesus, Paul was able to see beyond the cultural barriers and help them see the larger mystery. He used their culture to transcend all culture with the message of Jesus.

This passion for being with Jesus on the mission field spills over into the congregation in such a way that innovation is more the result of the congregational environment than anything else. Passionate leaders create such an environment, especially the lead pastor. The lead pastor exemplifies the innovation and takes some risks. These leaders never stifle an innovating moment even if they're not sure it will fly. I remember returning from vacation to find a note on my office door from one of the preaching pastors—*"Bill, wear blue jeans Sunday morning to worship. We are going to wear them all summer."* At the time I thought it was a dumb idea that would cause lots of trouble, but I went along. Today, it is normal dress for many postmodern churches.

Pastors should spend at least a fourth of their time with non-Christians and unconnected people, exploring their world. I made it a practice to visit places like bars, nightclubs, city hall, movies, or groups such as Lions, Realtors, and Developers. At one point I had a second job during some of the summer months (in the early years) so that I would learn the world of business. If you are in a stuck congregation, it's likely that you are surrounded by unimaginative, non-innovative people who worship the mantra *"We've never done it that way before, and we ain't going to start now!"*

I've seen several congregations intentionally send out teams into certain parts of the community that they would normally avoid, in order to do an amateur sociological study of a group of people. One congregation sent a group of people to live on the streets over a weekend to learn what it's like to be homeless. Another congregation did focus groups with a cross-cultural group of people. Another congregation sent a team into the bars around their church to see what issues were common from bar to bar. Early Christianity grew rapidly because it crossed all cultural and social barriers. No one was considered untouchable. Much of modern-day Christianity is too tied to one particular culture. It is time we opened wide the doors once again.

So what are some other ways you can foster innovation? Here are a few lessons I've learned along the way.

- Innovation happens most often when it is a stated part of your Value Statement and taught and encouraged as often as possible.

- Make heroes out of those leaders who attempt new ministries, and you will have more people experimenting with new ways to enhance the mission.

- Learn how to analyze the demographics of the area surrounding your congregation. Innovative congregations always know their customer better than stuck congregations. Each year, the congregation where I served did a demographic study from a group called Percept.[2] From that study, we always discovered new possibilities for ministry.

- Always point attention to new ministries and leaders who attempt new ministries, even if they are failures. 3M has a policy of allowing each employee fifteen percent of her or his time to work on projects of her or his own choosing. This has led 3M to be one of the most innovative companies in the world. While I was pastor of Colonial Hills, all of our staff were asked to designate ten percent of their time to whatever project they wanted. This led us to be one of the most innovative churches in our area of the country.

- Work around the edges of your religious group (denomination, association, or network) because innovation has less resistance there. You will never find the status quo at the edge, nor will you hear "we've never done it that way before." Maximize your edges by reading in areas outside of your discipline, attending events not put on by your denomination, networking with pastors in other traditions, talking with your kids, visiting new web sites, or going places you would not normally go.

- Challenge your leaders beyond what they think they are capable of achieving. Innovation is often the result of an over-sized vision or goal. Another way to think of this is to think, "The only place to find God working is among the impossible."

- Throw out as many new ideas as possible even if some sound stupid to you. They may spark insight in someone else. The more ideas running around in people's heads, the more innovation. Innovation is a team sport. The more people bat ideas around, the more innovation occurs.

- Honor risk, and don't be afraid of mistakes. Failure is just part of the culture of innovation. Accept it and become stronger. There is power in a big failure if you are looking for the lessons. Help people feel as if it is safe to talk freely about their mistakes. See mistakes as stepping-stones to future ministries. Always ask, *"What have we learned from this experience that will serve our mission in the future?"* You may even want to base some of the paid servants' salary on how many new things they try, even if they lead to failures.

- Give people all the information they want about what is happening in the congregation. People seldom innovate when they do not understand. They are also reluctant to try new things when they don't understand why the change is taking place.

- Focus groups can help you identify ministry possibilities that you might not otherwise consider.[3]

- Leaders must remove as many barriers to innovation as possible. Often the biggest barriers are Controllers, apathetic, or tired people. Encourage your paid and unpaid servants to have regular sabbaticals from whatever they are doing. Paid servants should be expected to have regular prayer and devotional time. Pure daydreaming and waiting on God are essential to innovation. As soon as you perfect what you are doing, move on to something else. Don't hang on too long to something working well. Keep looking for ways to improve what you're doing or how to move to the next level. The old adage, "don't let go of what you've got until you have something new to grab hold of," simply does not mean much in a turbulent environment. Realize that in times of great change whatever works well today is the seedbed for tomorrow's failure. It is true: if it ain't broke, fix it.

• Use the *Why* word a lot. Curiosity is an essential part of innovation.

• A valuable resource on innovation is *Diffusion of Innovations*, by Everett M. Rogers.[4] It is one of the classic books on change and how innovation actually causes change within a system. Although much of the book is highly technical, church leaders looking for solid handles to effecting change will find this book more than helpful. Some will want to skip the technical and focus on Chapter One and the excellent summaries at the end of each chapter. With minimal adaptation, this book is easily applied to the local congregation.

1995

• Finally, listen to your instinct, not your critics. The first twenty years of my ministry I received a lot of criticism from all fronts. I was told I was doing everything all wrong, even though the congregation was growing faster than any other congregation in the entire area. All along, I felt in my heart that what I was doing was what God wanted done, but surely my peers couldn't all be wrong. There was a short period of time when I listened to them too much, and it caused me to waste some valuable years. However, it soon became clear that what I was doing was causing my church to grow and what they were advocating was causing their churches to decline. So, I followed my heart and tuned them out. Now, I find it hard to stay home enough because so many people consider what I am advocating to be the way to the future.

Embedding The DNA

Without the DNA firmly embedded throughout the leaders, the permission-giving, innovative congregation never materializes. Embedding the DNA can happen in many ways, but it usually includes the following minimum:

- All of the paid and unpaid staff, but the lead pastor in particular, are the guardians and proclaimers of the DNA.

- New members are taught the DNA and expected to embrace it before joining.

- All leaders understand, seek to live out, and teach the DNA.

- All leaders gather each month to explore the DNA afresh, to be reminded of its importance to their mission, and to share in the joys of those who have seen the DNA enhanced during the month.

- Every decision-making group evaluates their decisions in light of the DNA.

- Anything that violates the DNA is immediately dropped.

- Anyone who is not comfortable with the DNA is encouraged to find a congregation in which he or she can be fulfilled.

For more on embedding the DNA see Thomas Bandy, *Moving Off the Map* and *Christian Chaos*.

Three mutually reinforcing processes are at the heart of this DNA— Invite, Grow, and Send. (*See* **Figure Seven**.)

Figure Seven

58

The goal of the Inviting phase is to provide safe entry points into the congregation where people experience authentic community and are either converted or assimilated into the congregation, depending on their prior spiritual journey. The public is invited to take a look at what people are experiencing in your midst and are introduced to Jesus. An Inviting congregation has:

- An intentional process to assimilate people into the community of faith,

- Methodology and corporate environment that are culturally relevant,

- A community life that is healthy, loving, caring, and is without major conflict,

- A passion to ask friends in to experience authentic Christian community,

- Many entry points into the community of faith, which are familiar and safe to people who have never been in a congregation.

As a result, persons are invited to participate in:

- A personal and corporate relationship with Jesus Christ,

- An environment of trust, constant growth and change,

- A community where persons routinely experience personal growth and/or find new life.

The goal of the Growing phase is to find a place in the Body of Christ and to become empowered to make disciples who make disciples, by finding authentic community, understanding, and enthusiastically upholding the Mission, Vision, and Value Statements, discovering their gifts and discerning their place in the body, understanding the present ministries, and in time assuming spiritual leadership. Growth means that:

- The theology and teaching are biblically sound.

- Persons are free to follow their spiritual passion as long as it enhances the consensus mission of the congregation.

- Leaders go out of their way to remove barriers to the priesthood of the believer.

- Everything is based on where persons are in their spiritual journey, not where the church needs them to be.

- Leaders value other persons the way God values them.

- The congregations have fishing pools (large and small events) in which to discover new leaders.

As a result persons grow:

- Closer to God,

- Deeper, healthier relationships,

- In their understanding of Scripture,

- In how to birth their God-given gifts,

- In how to grow other leaders,

- In their prayer life,

- In their understanding of how to minister and be a servant.

The goal of the Sending phase is for all Christians to become ministers of Jesus Christ for the purpose of using their gifts on the mission field to make disciples and change the world, instead of serving the institution by serving on committees. Send means:

- Persons are commissioned to use their faith in the secular world as well as among the congregation.

- The focus of the leaders is outward rather than inward.

As a result, persons are sent into the mission field to:

- Deploy their gifts on behalf of others,

- Take responsibility for their life and the lives of others,

- Invite others to experience the love and trust of God in a permission-giving congregation.

Innovate Boldly

If you are going to experiment with new ways to do ancient ministry, go for the audacious innovations. Small innovations are little more than tinkering and probably don't accomplish anything other than to keep the Controllers in an uproar and deflate the Dreamers.

Remember, innovation is not about skills; it is about passion for ministry. I believe that anyone with a deep passion for mission can explore more of the edges of congregational life than they think. If you feel in your gut that there must be more to ministry than you are experiencing at the moment, start the journey and trust your instinct. You can always find another church if it does not work.

1. For more on the subject see William Easum and Thomas Bandy, *Growing Spiritual Redwoods* (Nashville: Abingdon Press, 1997).
2. http://www.perceptnet.com/
3. For more on focus groups see http://www.easumbandy.com/FAQS/focus_groups.htm.
4. *Diffusion of Innovations*, Everett M. Rogers (New York: Free Press, 1995), 519 pages paperback, $32.95. Obtain from The Free Press, A Division of Simon & Schuster, Inc., 1230 Avenue of the Americas, New York, NY 10020.

Chapter 5
The Foundations of
Transformation and Innovation

In times of traumatic, discontinuous transition, anything considered to be *classic* is at best suspicious and should be re-evaluated. Such is the case with the classic view of change.

The Classic View of Change No Longer Works

The classic view of change, as popularized by Kurt Lewin, involves three steps.[1] First, someone, whom we will call the change agent, *unfreezes* the status quo. In a congregation, this is usually the pastor. Next, the change agent makes a change of some magnitude that causes people to think and act differently from the past. Third, the change agent *refreezes* the organization. This view of change worked well in the slow, evolutionary past. But it's a recipe for failure in the present world of rapid change and discontinuity.

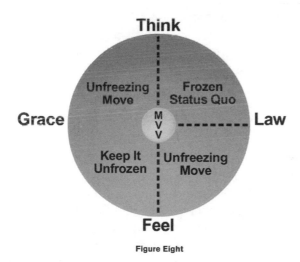

Figure Eight

Sphere Three congregations never refreeze the organization. (See Figure Eight.) Instead, the Dreamers, now turned leaders, cause the next unfreezing move to occur without refreezing the organization so that change is built into the fabric of congregational life. The leaders build momentum upon momentum, resulting in a constantly innovative environment. Freezing occurs only when a congregation moves into Sphere Four for a breather and stays there for as short a period of time as possible.

In times of rapid change, refreezing causes leaders to get too far behind the change curve, and they lose momentum as the rate of change continues to accelerate. Yet, in spite of the acceleration in the rate of change over the past forty years, the classic view of change still dominates organizational theory. As a result, most established congregations avoid as many changes as possible; thus, they lose momentum and can't keep up with the rapid pace of transition.

New Process of Change

- Unfreeze
- Make Major Change
- Do not Refreeze
- Unfreeze Again

Unfreezing Moves

Stuck and unstuck congregations never become unstuck or innovative without someone making an "unfreezing move." In a stuck system, an unfreezing move occurs when an individual or group challenges the status quo in such a way that the system story becomes destabilized, at least for a moment, by catching the Controllers off guard and giving the Dreamers a glimmer of hope. In an innovative congregation, an unfreezing move occurs when a congregation intentionally enters a totally new phase, level, or direction of ministry. The more stuck a congregation is, the more traumatic the unfreezing move. The more innovative the congregation is, the less likely the unfreezing move will even be noticed. Still, both congregational spheres require unfreezing moves because it is normal for people quickly to become comfortable with the status quo even in the most innovative congregations. Beginning in Chapter Six, I will discuss the key unfreezing moves.

Keep in mind that just because an unfreezing move is made it doesn't mean that the system story is transformed. It simply has been destabilized, for the moment. For years, it will return to the status quo if given the slightest opportunity.

Almost any unfreezing move that successfully destabilizes the systems story during Sphere One or Two can be expected to cause any or all of the following results:

- Relationships will be broken, resulting in a loss of people, not all of whom are Controllers. So if you're going to make an unfreezing move, be sure to inform your Dreamers that a loss of people will most likely occur before any positive growth is experienced.

- There will be a substantial shifting of responsibilities and discovery of additional new leaders.

- Confusion will exist for a period of time.

When an unfreezing move is made in an innovative congregation, the following can be expected:

- The climate for more innovation is increased.

- Paid servants usually need to adjust some of their habits and often require additional training or equipping.

- Confusion among those on the fringes is minimal.

- Momentum increases, resulting in more personal and corporate growth

The three keys to making an unfreezing move are knowing:

- How to find the appropriate unfreezing move;

- How to focus on the unfreezing move;

- How to align around the unfreezing move.

We must now look at these three keys.

Finding the Appropriate Unfreezing Move

Nine unfreezing moves are at the disposal of Dreamers who are ready to function as leaders. These are listed in Figure Nine in the order of their *chronological* importance. When the unfreezing moves are accomplished in this order, transformation or innovation happens easier and without as much resistance. However, Dreamers can begin the change process anywhere along the way, especially in Sphere Three and Four congregations without Controllers or major dysfunction. The change is merely easier if the unfreezing moves are in the order suggested below.

UNFREEZING MOVES

- A Solid Community of Faith

- Owned and Managed DNA

- Indigenous Worship

- Lay Mobilization

- Redemptive Missional Opportunity

- Organized Around DNA

- Staffing

- Logistics of Parking and Facilities

- Finances

Figure Nine

Do not conclude that these unfreezing moves always occur separate from one another. (*See* **Figure Ten**.) Each one mutually reinforces the other. When taken in the order in which they are listed, the effect of the next unfreezing move is never as traumatic. Stuck congregations usually must focus on one unfreezing move at a time. Innovative congregations may have several unfreezing moves occurring at the same time. For example: a stuck congregation usually must focus most of its attention on freeing the congregation from the grip of the Controllers. Getting rid of the ongoing conflict has to occur before it does anything else. Once that is done, it has been so long since anything new has happened that doing many new things at once can stop the transformation because it sends the more healthy leaders into shock. So it is better to make one unfreezing move at a time in the stuck or early going of becoming unstuck. On the other hand, because innovative congregations have more trust and have become accustomed to change, they can be starting alternative forms of worship while changing the basic organizational structure as well as implementing a major new ministry. Congregations that attempt to discover and articulate their purpose or mission without developing spiritual giants, trust, and eliminating the major ongoing conflict, will find it extremely difficult to arrive at a workable and biblical purpose or mission.

Figure Ten

Notice in Figure Ten that all of the unfreezing moves revolve around the Mission, Vision, Values, and Beliefs of the congregation. These are the DNA, or the heart, of innovative congregations in Spheres Three or Four. Discovering and embedding this DNA throughout the leadership is the most important thing a congregation ever does. However, you will notice it is not listed first in chronological order.

Therefore, discovering the appropriate unfreezing move is crucial to a smooth transformation. No single way exists to find the right unfreezing move. For the last two decades of my ministry as a pastor, I used what I now call The Complete Ministry Audit.[2] It assisted me in seeing trends before they became obstacles that might stop the congregation moving forward. Only once during that time did the scope of our ministry fail to increase. Over the years, I have continued to revise and update this tool. Tom Bandy uses a tool called Church Mission Assessment, which he has used with much success in his consulting ministry.[3] Many other such tools exist. I encourage you to find one that best fits your ministry.

Focus

Focus is a willingness on the part of a congregation to do whatever is necessary to achieve the appropriate unfreezing move. In both a stuck and unstuck congregation, focus requires paid and unpaid staff to spend eighty percent of their time on the appropriate unfreezing move, especially in the beginning.

The ability to focus is a major challenge in stuck congregations because their understanding of how God expects leaders to function is flawed. Every stuck congregation with whom I have worked sees its pastor and staff as hired guns to do its bidding and to take care of the membership and the institution. Stuck congregations never seem to understand that the biblical role of leadership is to equip the saints for the work of ministry (Ephesians 4:11–12). They want their pastor and staff to do everything for everyone, even if they are willing to attempt an unfreezing move. But so much is asked of their paid leaders, most of which is unbiblical, that it becomes impossible for them to focus eighty percent of their time on anything.

It's hard to gain focus when everyone in the congregation wants something from the lead pastor.

Biblical illiteracy and spiritual malnourishment are the greatest barriers to being able to achieve any unfreezing move well enough for congregations to become unstuck. I have seen pastors burn out, drop out, and go through divorces from burning the candle at both ends, trying to do everything for the congregation and simultaneously attempt an unfreezing move. This inability to burn the candle at both ends is one of the primary reasons, as we will see later, that the first unfreezing move is growing a group of spiritual giants who can give biblical leadership to the unfreezing moves.

The greatest obstacle to focus in innovative congregations is competition or jealousy among paid or unpaid leaders. Over time, a feeling may arise that what one group of leaders does is more important than what some other leaders are doing. Different groups begin to vie for attention or money or facilities instead of considering what is best for the congregation and the enhancement of the DNA. Outside speaking opportunities and publishing contracts of some of the paid staff can exacerbate the jealousies. If this happens, the leaders affected should literally repent of their pride, or, if pride and arrogance expands, they should be asked to resign from leadership. To allow them to continue their superior behavior is a good way for the church to slip into Sphere One without ever going through Sphere Four. This happens most often at the arrival of a new lead pastor who is not secure enough to allow innovation or exposure to bubble up from any place in the congregation. In effect, the lead pastor becomes the ultimate Controller; trust is lost; effective paid staff leave; and unpaid staff members seek another congregation in which to serve.

Alignment

Alignment occurs when a congregation puts all of its resources into the unfreezing move. At a minimum, alignment means that the necessary time, energy, money, and paid and unpaid leaders are aligned around the unfreezing move. At its best, alignment also means that anything that hinders the success of the unfreezing move is eliminated, and anything that will enhance the unfreezing move is added. In a stuck congregation, this often means the following: the reallocation of the budget so that the unfreezing move is fully funded; the replacement of some paid or unpaid staff or the addition of some new paid or unpaid leaders; and a willingness to ensure that everything the congregation does helps make the unfreezing a reality. In an innovative congregation it means that paid and unpaid leaders are on board with the overall DNA of the congregation, understand the importance of the unfreezing move, and wholeheartedly support it. It only takes one key leader to be out of alignment, especially if that person is a paid staff person, to stifle the mission or squelch the unfreezing move.

Alignment is impossible if just one of the paid or unpaid leaders is not on the same page.

A good image of bad alignment is that of a stagecoach drawn by a team of horses at full gallop. Suddenly, one horse—it doesn't matter which one—decides to sit down. What happens to the stagecoach isn't pretty. Congregations have the same experience when any key leader decides to balk and go a different direction than the discovered unfreezing move.

Some will see focus and alignment as dictatorial. And it is dictatorial, in a way, though the DNA dictates the alignment, rather than an individual despot. The DNA is the consensus of the leadership that is arrived at only after much prayer, study, and discernment. (Leaders in a Sphere One or Two congregation where trust has been absent for a long time will have a hard time buying into the fact that congregations can arrive at consensus.) Some may say that focus and alignment are exclusive, because it appears that alignment does not permit diversity, so that all voices have equal authority. I readily admit that alignment is exclusive in one way: It excludes the spiritually immature Controllers who wish to have everything established to their liking, and thus preserve the status quo. Focus and alignment are not some arbitrary decision of the pastor or paid staff. They stem from discerning the implications of the consensus DNA of the congregation.

Two System Stories

Two stories will help us see the importance of taking the unfreezing moves in the order I have suggested.

In the early years of my consulting experience, I worked with a small, dying congregation in the Midwest that had one worship service with about seventy-five people on an average Sunday. Among this number were only four youth under the age of sixteen. The rest of the congregation was at least the age of fifty. The leaders said they wanted to reach out to the large group of young adults in the community around the church. I took them at their word and proceeded to help them design a way to reach this group. My primary recommendation was to begin a second worship service that would be designed to reach young adults. I recommended a band, praise music, and singers with microphones.

The church responded by doing everything I recommended, and within eighteen months was averaging over one hundred and seventy-five total in the two services. About that time they invited me to come back for a second visit, which I thought would be an exciting opportunity to help them make another unfreezing move. Instead, I refereed a fight. The old-timers were bent out of shape because their worship service had dwindled to forty people, and the four young people were attending the new service. They were mad because the new service was larger and contained a number of new young families.

I left the church shaking my head in disbelief. They got what they asked for: The congregation was growing and getting younger, and yet they were tearing each other apart. A few months after this second consultation with them, the small handful of Controllers decided to stop the new worship service and go back to the one traditional service so that both young and old could worship together. Within two years the Dreamers left and the church closed. What's wrong with this picture?

For the past thirty years, church consultants have known that the easiest and fastest way to grow a traditional church is to start a new worship service designed to reach the generation of Baby Boomers. However, if the church is conflicted, or does not have clarity of purpose, conflict always seems to emerge around this new type of service, especially if it succeeds. It was from experiences like this that I begin to see the importance of the chronological order of the nine unfreezing moves.

If a congregation is conflicted even a little, or is not clear about its mission, any new ministry that upsets Controllers results in major conflict that often leads to the loss of the pastor and the elimination of the new ministry, thus returning to Sphere One. The confusion and angst of the Controllers is too great for them not to respond with all of their accumulated power.

On the other hand, healthy and innovative congregations that know where they are going have little conflict over starting new forms of worship. This experience taught me that the first two unfreezing moves must be the development of a solid community of faith and an owned and managed Mission, Vision, and Value Statement. The word owned means that the leadership has ownership in the agreed upon Mission, Vision, and Values of the congregation. The word *managed* means that every decision is evaluated in light of the Mission, Vision, and Values. *Managed* is not used in the sense of micromanage.

The second systems story comes from my own experience as the pastor of a turnaround congregation. In the early months of turning around the congregation in which I remained for twenty-four years, the leaders wanted to focus only on the lack of money. Their concern was real, even if it was misdirected. The bank that held the note on the debt had given the church a three-month notice of foreclosure. The leaders had a right to be concerned about the lack of money, but it was only a symptom of the real problem.

During my first month as pastor, I went to dozens of meetings, each one focusing on the lack of money. Finally, one day I'd had enough and said, "I'm not coming to another meeting if all you're going to talk about is money. It's time we quit worrying about money and begin asking why there isn't more money than we know how to handle. Why aren't people willing to give? Could it be there's nothing here that is worth our giving?"

You could have heard a pin drop. But then it began to soak in with the leaders. Two meetings later, we realized that the issue wasn't the lack of money. The issue was that there wasn't any reason for anyone new to participate in our lifeless congregation. The more this realization soaked in, the more willing we were to make radical changes. It was in those early years of my ministry in this congregation that I learned two things. One, money is never the issue; lack of faith is the issue. That's why I put money at the bottom of the list of unfreezing moves. And two, the more discontented people become, the more open they are to transformation.

Unfreezing Opportunities

Dreamers have at least six major opportunities to make an unfreezing move. These opportunities occur when:

- Your innovative congregation has just experienced a major breakthrough of a new ministry, and everyone is excited. Rather than taking a breather, move on to the next innovation. Make sure that the innovations sooner or later cover all nine of the unfreezing moves. You will find over time that you will revisit these nine moves over and over as they morph in complexity with the growth of the congregation and the changes in culture.

- A stuck congregation experiences a serious crisis that causes the Controllers to be willing to allow a new direction to be attempted. Often this is a serious inability to pay the basic bills.

- The congregation is flooded by a substantial number of new participants who insist on getting more out of their faith than is presently being allowed. Often, this is the result of the arrival of a new pastor who single-handedly brings in enough new people to upset the balance of power, thus freeing up the system story. This unfreezing move presents a much longer window of opportunity to make an unfreezing move. This unfreezing move also represents the least amount of vulnerability for the pastor. Therefore, pastors should not listen to those who tell them not to do anything during their first year, other than getting to know the members. That is deadly advice.

- A new set of leaders is placed into power. This is one of the most stable ways to make an unfreezing move. However, it requires an intentional and sometimes long-term (usually a year or more) underground-type effort to equip a new set of leaders, and to do whatever is necessary to move them into the primary power positions. Often, this is the most difficult form of unfreezing move because of the watchful eye of the Controllers. This unfreezing move seldom happens without the pastor becoming extremely vulnerable if the unfreezing move doesn't work.

- A major Controller dies. Often this death leaves a vacuum as well as a brief moment when a new person or group can give new direction. It should be noted that this usually provides only a small window of time in which an unfreezing move can be made.

- A new endowment is received that is earmarked for the rebirth of the church. The problem with this opportunity is that the change agent usually has to wait until the congregation closes before making an unfreezing move.

- One or more of the Controllers is converted. From a purely spiritual standpoint, this is the most repentant approach, which reminds us of Paul on the Damascus Road. It requires much prayer and hard work. It also is the least likely unfreezing move to occur due to the hardness of the Controller's hearts. By now you are aware that we are talking about a form of spiritual warfare. If you are in a stuck congregation and are naive on this point, the odds are long that you will not succeed as a change agent.

Before Attempting the First Unfreezing Move

Many Dreamers in stuck congregations often find it harder than they thought to change the systems story. Many invest years in trying to change the system only to give up in order to preserve their own spirituality and sanity. So, before attempting an unfreezing move in a stuck congregation decide:

• What objective measurements you are going to use to help you decide where to begin the change process and to determine if you are making progress. Again, I suggest the *Permission-giving Readiness Inventory*. It will tell you where you need to put the most work.

• The amount of sweat equity you are willing to invest. Keep in mind that the personality and gifts of the leader have some bearing on the length of time it takes a church to move through a transition, and the amount of success the leader will ensure. The higher your mercy gifts, the longer it will take. Give yourself at least three to five years to know if the transition is taking place, and monitor your own feelings to see if you are personally going to be able to handle the stress. If you haven't moved out of Sphere One into Sphere Three by then, you probably won't, so you might as well move on to a more open congregation.

A Word of Wisdom for Leaders

Like Peter trying to learn to walk on water, you must take the first step out of the boat if you want to follow Jesus into the mission field.

Transformation or innovation seldom happens accidentally. Someone must step out of the system long enough to name the systems story, and then make an unfreezing move even if it is the wrong move. In stuck congregations, the initial unfreezing move can be as simple as gathering and equipping a small group of

Dreamers, or it can be as traumatic as replacing all of the present leaders in a sudden coup. In innovative congregations, making an unfreezing move can be as simple as applying lessons learned from previous mistakes to a new ministry, or as traumatic as taking the stand that "if it ain't broke, we need to fix it." But in both cases making the unfreezing move would be much like Peter learning to walk on water. To do so, he had to take that first step out of the boat. Is it time you stepped out of the boat and joined Jesus on the mission field? That is the subject of the remaining chapters.

---

1. Much of Lewin's early writings are out of print. To read more about Lewin's work, see http://www.solonline.org/res/wp/10006.html and http://www.managementfirst.com/professional_organisations/information_man agement.htm.
2. William M. Easum, *The Complete Ministry Audit* (Nashville: Abingdon Press, 1994). See lifecycles 1.
3. Thomas G. Bandy, *Facing Reality: A Tool for Congregational Mission Assessment* (Nashville: Abingdon Press, 2001).

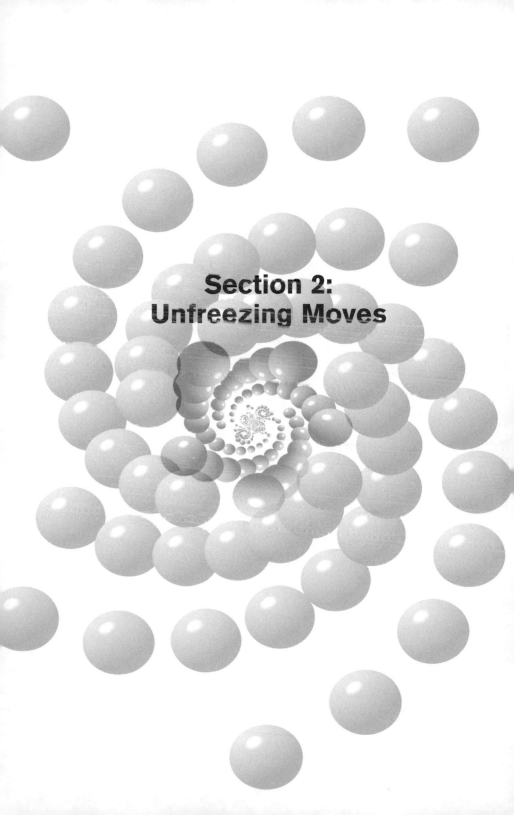

Section 2:
Unfreezing Moves

Chapter 6
The Two Foundational
Unfreezing Moves

This section is designed to help you determine what unfreezing move you need to make in transforming a stuck congregation or developing an innovative congregation. The particular unfreezing move is described and a list of statements is provided for each unfreezing move to help you determine if you need to begin with that unfreezing move. Answer each statement based on how you feel the congregation behaves, not on how you wish it behaved. These questions will serve you well only if you are brutally honest with your answers. A score of 1 means that you feel the statement totally describes the behavior of your congregation, and a score of 10 means that you feel the statement totally misrepresents the behavior of your congregation. When you finish, average the scores. If the average score is between 1 and 2, you leaders are ready to move on to the next unfreezing move. If your average score is between 3 and 4, it is questionable whether you should move on or work on this unfreezing move. If your average score is 5 or more, you definitely need to spend more time working on that particular unfreezing move.

Here's an easy formula to remember:

Green Light: 1–2   **Yellow Light:** 3–4   **Red Light:** 5 or above

Keep in mind the following advice as you read this section:

- The unfreezing moves are listed in the order that they make the next unfreezing move easier and less painful to accomplish.

- Additional "how-to" resources are included in the resource section in Appendix B.

- Unless you are already an unstuck and innovative congregation, you will probably work on one of the unfreezing moves at a time. When you accomplish that unfreezing move, you can refer back to this book to assist you in your next move. If you are unstuck and innovative already, you can work on several unfreezing moves at the same time. This tool may become one of your constant companions for several years.

- Should you decide that ongoing coaching would help, you have several options. You can join our EBA Community and participate in our online seminars; participate in one of our free listservs at www.easumbandy.com (I monitor those listservs daily.); or receive one-on-one coaching from any one of our consultants by emailing us at easum@easumbandy.com. You can also have one of our consultants work with you onsite.

Unfreezing Move One: A Solid Community of Faith

John 17:20-22

"In the postmodern landscape, community is our first and best apologetic."—*Todd Hahn*

Spiritual Leadership

Most congregations have been adrift for so long that it is unlikely that the handful of spiritually hungry Dreamers have any solid biblical foundation. Before they can lead and/or replace the Deciders/Controllers, they must be grounded in a solid understanding of how spiritual leaders and faithful congregations function.

Do not downplay the importance of developing spiritual giants before trying to transform a congregation. The most important issue in transforming a congregation is the spiritual dimension of the leadership, no matter how much the leaders know about change principles. As we saw in Chapter Three, the desire for control is a spiritual issue, the root of which is the sin of self-centeredness. Congregational transformation can occur only when the leaders let go of their self-centered approach to faith and allow Christ and his wishes to become the center of their faith. You need to develop spiritual giants who have a radical devotion to Jesus Christ.

Spiritual explosion takes place after a congregation has been in Sphere Three long enough for spiritual leaders to spend most of their time coaching other leaders. The goal of this coaching in all four spheres is to grow empowered servants who use their talent and gifts on behalf of building up the Body of Christ. Often, unstuck congregations have to spend several years in Sphere Three doing de-programming, retraining, and simple remedial Bible work and spiritual development among the potential new leaders. Over time, innovative congregations spend more and more time and money on the training and equipping of their spiritual leaders.

In the first month of my twenty-four-year pastorate, I called out a group of individuals based on the life I saw them leading and the gleam in their eye when I cast my vision. I met with them each week for a couple of hours for a period of about eight months. We read and reread the Book of Acts and asked God to help us become like the church depicted in Acts. When I thought they were ready, we went out into the neighborhood and asked what people needed that they weren't getting from churches in the area. One out of six households said they needed quality childcare during the week (this was 1969). This small group of twelve people formulated a strategic map based on all they had learned over the eight months from their Bible study and sharing, from me, and from the input of the community at large. Using this map, together we moved our stuck and dying congregation to one of the most innovative congregations in Texas. This transformation would never have gotten off the ground without the development of those twelve deeply committed Christians who were willing to risk friendship and income for the sake of the Great Commission.

These statements will help you analyze the spiritual strength of your leaders.

❑ Our leaders can articulate the implications of their relationship with Jesus Christ without sounding like bigots.

❑ The Scriptures are embodied in the daily life of our leaders.

❑ Called and gifted unpaid leaders teach most of our Bible studies.

❑ Our leaders appear to be growing more like Jesus.

❑ Our leaders serve outside the congregation as much as they serve within the institution.

❑ All of our leaders are in an accountability or small group.

❑ Our leaders function as a team.

❑ When our leaders pray, lives are touched by the presence of the Holy Spirit.

❑ Our leaders offer to pray for others on a regular basis.

❑ Our leaders have a regular prayer life.

❑ Our leaders are always open to new ways of doing ministry.

❑ Our leaders serve out of gratitude for what God has done in their lives.

❑ Our unpaid leaders have the skills needed to take greater responsibility for the ministries of the church.

Our average score is:

1–2: Green Light   **3–4:** Yellow Light   **5 or above:** Red Light

Function Around Trust

Spiritual giants form a bond with other spiritual giants, which fosters a level of trust that raises them above having to be in control, because they can trust one another and the movement of God's Spirit. Is it any wonder that the need for a caring, loving, and accepting biblical community of faith is the top priority for unsticking a congregation or for being a constantly innovative congregation?

Here is a list of questions to determine how much trust resides in your leaders.

❑ Our leaders are never concerned if ministries or programs happen without their knowledge or approval.

❑ Our leaders assume that the actions of other leaders are always on behalf of the good of the congregation, even if those actions do not interest them.

❑ Our spiritual leaders are in one-to-one, hands-on ministry each week.

❑ A significant part of all meetings is set aside for prayer and discernment.

❑ A climate of hospitality and love is found whenever our congregation gets together, even at official meetings.

❑ Our leaders appear to have fun when they are involved in ministry.

❑ People are free to begin new ministries based on their gifts and talents without having to ask permission from a centralized authority.

Our average score is:

1–2: Green Light   **3–4:** Yellow Light   **5 or above:** Red Light

No Major, Ongoing Conflict

Conflicted congregations never enter Sphere Three because the number-one thing non-Christians need is a loving, accepting community in which they can experience authentic love and community. I'm not referring to occasional disagreements. Every congregation has these. The issue here is ongoing verbal and political abuse that results in a dysfunctional leadership and congregation. Fear dominates everything. People are afraid of new ideas, new people, new ministries. People walk on eggshells when certain people are present. A handful of people bully the congregation for years. Often you can tell if a congregation is dysfunctional if it has routinely run off pastor after pastor and is known as a "pastor-eating congregation." A congregation experiencing major, ongoing conflict must pause in its attempts at transformation and deal with the situation.

A Word to Leaders Under Siege

Trying to transform a congregation and dealing with Controllers can be deadly business, turning the hopes of leaders/Dreamers into a living nightmare. When this happens, leaders must rely on two things: the power of their call and the knowledge that Jesus gave his all for what they are going through. It also helps to know that you are actually fighting evil. These people are not against you; they are against being the church, against everything Jesus stood for. So don't despair. They can't hurt you. If you are called of God, then God will take care of you. You will find another place to serve if you get kicked out. So don't concentrate on the Controllers; concentrate on the eyes of the Dreamers who are opening up to the possibility of new life in Christ. Focus on that. Remember, most of the opposition isn't evil; they just don't get it, yet. So plod on.

Here is a list to determine if your congregation is conflicted.

❏ Our endowments and savings are never used to support the basic budget of the congregation. This money can be used to begin new ministries to connect with the outside world or hire new paid servants for a short time.

❏ Our church is free from power cliques.

❏ No individual or group of two or three persons has the power to derail things that the majority wants.

❏ Reaching new people is more important than caring for our members.

❏ Our church has a history of following through on new ideas.

❏ Our key leadership is willing to share its power with those who are not in leadership.

❑ Paying the bills is the least important thing we can do.

❑ The roll of our paid servants is to equip the congregation for ministry.

❑ Our congregation is known for its hospitality and health in the surrounding community.

❑ New worship styles can be added without much difficulty.

❑ Someone on the paid staff knows how much money everyone gives.

❑ Everyone serves based on his or her gifts instead of the needs of the congregation.

❑ Change is part of our culture, and most of our people handle it well

❑ Our church leaders believe that people doing the actual ministry should make the majority of the decisions that affect how they do their ministry.

❑ Our Finance and Trustee Committees exist to serve the needs of those trying to implement ministry.

❑ Our official meetings never feel angry or hostile.

Our average score is:

1–2: Green Light   **3–4:** Yellow Light   **5 or above:** Red Light

A Desire to Connect With the Outside World

The heart of a solid community of faith beats for the unconnected of the world. The leaders live to be light, salt, and leaven to those around them and to the world. The entire biblical story depicts God's blessing of God's people so that they may in turn bless others. Failure to be a blessing to others is the subject of several parables that Jesus leveled at Israel's refusal to be a blessing to the nations of the world (Matt. 21:43).

The congregations best able to reach the unconnected are those that have wrestled with the question, what is it about our relationship with Jesus that the world cannot live without experiencing? Not only do they know the answer, but they are willing to do anything to share what they have experienced. Leaders in Sphere Three congregations never entertain questions such as: Is our church big enough? Shouldn't we take better care of our current members before we try to reach any more people? Instead they ask: Does everyone around us know God? These leaders are always looking outside to the mission field.

Here is a list of statements to determine where your leaders are with respect toward reaching out to non-Christians and unconnected Christians. (Proselytizing is never acceptable in organic movements.)

❑ All of our ministries have an outreach component that is an entry point into the life of the congregation.

❑ All of our small groups and/or Sunday School classes have a monthly mission.

❑ The people responsible for finances ask how each item will enhance the DNA and improve the ability of the congregation to reach the unreached.

❑ When our leaders pray in public most of their prayers are for the non-Christians with whom they have a relationship.

❑ A sizeable portion of our budget is designed to equip our leaders to connect with the outside world.

Our average score is:

1–2: Green Light   **3–4:** Yellow Light   **5 or above:** Red Light

Unfreezing Move Two:
Discovering and Articulating the DNA

Acts 2:42

In Sphere Three and Four congregations, it is imperative for the leadership and some of the congregation to have a clear understanding of the purpose of the congregation. Congregations will express their DNA in many ways. Some use Purpose Statements, and others use Core Values. For our purposes, we will refer to Mission, Vision, Values, and Belief.[1]

- A Mission Statement is a short, one-sentence explanation of what a congregation does. Example: "We exist for every person to become a minister of Jesus Christ."

- A Vision Statement is usually somewhat longer and describes how a congregation is going to carry out its mission. Example: "We will equip every person to become a minister of Jesus Christ by: providing them a permission-giving atmosphere in which they are encouraged to discover their God-given gifts; equipping them to deploy those gifts; and coaching them to effectively embed those gifts in the lives of others."

- A Values Statement is a document that sets the boundaries in which people are free to live out their God-given gifts and talents for the sake of the Body of Christ without going to a central committee to get permission. Example: "We value innovation, teams, and small groups that multiply, permission-giving, empowered servants, social justice, prayer, and diversity."

- A Belief Statement comes in many forms, depending on the denomination or background of the congregation, so I will not list any beliefs.

Think of these four documents as the DNA or the genetic code of a congregation. The DNA of every faithful congregation is focused some way on making disciples (Great Commission) and loving one another (Great Commandment), but every congregation carries out the DNA differently because of the different gene pool.

To be effective, these statements need to arise out of the deepest part of your leaders' spiritual life. They should reflect the unique way your church will attempt to faithfully follow Jesus into the mission field and to love one another. These documents will become your guide for all your decisions, time, money, staffing, ministries, and training. In essence, they become the leader of the congregation. Once these documents are in place, the role of the official body is no longer deciding what will or will not be done; but ensuring that the mission, vision, and values are upheld and enhanced throughout the congregation.

Once the DNA is articulated and agreed upon by the leadership, the DNA must be embedded into every leader at every level so that every decision is made based upon it enhancing the DNA—from saying yes to new ministries, to spending money, to hiring or terminating paid servants. In Sphere Three or Four, congregation leaders must thoroughly agree with and attempt to live out the DNA in their daily lives and in their mentoring of others.

As you can see, permission-giving is not an exercise in reckless abandonment, as most Controllers will try to tell you. The DNA guides and ensures that only things that enhance the DNA are permitted. You have predetermined boundaries and you have trained your leaders and embedded the DNA.[2]

Discovering a Biblically Sound and Culturally Relevant DNA

All systems have an embedded DNA; however, not all have one that is faithful to what it means to be the people of God. How a congregation is organized and spends its time and money shows if the DNA is faithful to the species known as Christian. The action of most Protestant congregations clearly shows that the vast majority of our congregations are little more than hospices or hospitals, if not clubs. Many congregations have a genetic code that is addicted to some form of cultural religion, which is far from biblical or spiritual.[3] The key to discovering, articulating, and embedding this DNA is to seek the direction and intervention of the divine wisdom that lurks within the hearts of Dreamers in the congregation who know that there must be more to Christianity than what they are tapping. Developing these individuals as the future spiritual leaders has already been noted as the first unfreezing move. If you have done that, this unfreezing move will be much easier.

Who Decides the DNA?

The number-one question asked by leaders wanting to make this unfreezing move is "Who decides on the DNA?" So, a couple of years ago, in an attempt to find some common denominators in the way DNA is determined in effective congregations, I interviewed Mike Foss, at Prince of Peace Lutheran at Burnsville, Minnesota (http://www.princeofpeaceonline.org/ and http://www.changingchurch.org/), Mike Slaughter at Ginghamsburg UMC at Tipp City, Ohio (http://ginghamsburg.org/), and Dick Wills at Christ Church UMC in Ft. Lauderdale, Florida (http://www.christchurchum.org/). All three of these are permission-giving congregations. To these interviews I added my own experience.

I discovered that we all did it differently. Mike Foss invited some key leaders to join him in a process. Mike Slaughter gathered, trained, and equipped a small band of disciples in his understanding of mission, and, during the second year of his tenure, put them into all of the power positions. Dick Wills had a life-altering experience that caused him to change his way of living and leading so much that it infected enough of the leaders that his new core values were adopted.[4] My first Sunday at the church where I was pastor for twenty-four years, I cast a vision, gathered a group of ready-to-go-disciples, and led them into transforming the congregation over the next eighteen months.[5]

However, some common denominators did arise from our experiences.

- DNA cannot be legislated by a committee or governing board. The process is usually initiated by the pastor and finely honed by the spiritual leaders. Congregational processes involving everyone usually result in watered-down documents. The fewer people involved in the process, the tighter and more biblical the DNA; the more people involved in the process, the easier it is to embed the DNA throughout the leadership. I recommend that only your most spiritually mature leaders take part in the process, at least toward the end when you are actually crafting the documents. It is folly to ask biblically illiterate people who do little more than serve on a committee or warm a pew to decide on God's mission for a congregation. If you have read Tom Bandy's book, *Moving Off the Map*, you may be a bit confused at this point because Tom suggests involving the whole congregation in this process. However, because of the amount of time involved in his model, you wind up toward the end with a handful of the more committed people involved in the end product. So, wherever you begin the process and if you do it with diligence, you will wind up with a small core of committed people doing the final draft.

- If the DNA is to become a shared vision, it must resonate deep down in the gut of the majority of the leadership or else it becomes a nightmare. The better the leader listens to the spiritual leaders in the congregation, the more effective the process will be.

- Sometimes the pastor must change before the congregation will change. The pastor must live out the DNA before others will.

- Congregations that discover their DNA find that people will re-up with more energy and time commitment, and then you are on your way to a permission-giving, innovative congregation.

- Small groups are almost always a part of the discovery period.

- Discovering and articulating the DNA is a spiritual thing; it is not another program or task to be completed. The more the process is saturated with prayer and discernment of what God wants, the more lasting the process.

- Everything must be grounded in Scripture.

- Leaders must lead.

- It is critical for all leaders, including paid staff, to be aligned with the DNA or get out of leadership. For paid staff that means leaving the congregation.

- When persons are held accountable in a system where previously there has been no accountability, expect a year or two of confusion, which may feel like another form of control.

- Churches that have high expectations of and requirements for their leaders weather the process much better.

- It is best to start the process the first Sunday as pastor of the church. Your start may be as simple as the message or as complex as beginning to gather around you those whose eyes lighted up when you preached your vision.

- Train a core group and put them in power ASAP.

- Do not flinch when obstinate people leave.

- Making change a part of the culture makes it easier for a congregation to be constantly innovative.

- If the pastor does not initiate the process, it seldom is effective. If the pastor cannot manage and guard the consensus DNA, over time it will fall by the wayside and be ineffective.

- How the DNA is discovered and articulated depends as much on the situation as the leader. In a new church start, it is best if the planting or founding pastor sets the mission, vision, and values, before inviting anyone in. If the congregation is very dysfunctional, my method or Mike Slaughter's approach works. If the congregation is free of conflict and has solid leadership, the method described by Tom Bandy in *Moving Off the Map* will work extremely well. (For those wanting a much more in-depth approach, see Thomas Bandy, *Moving Off the Map* from Abingdon.)

A Quick Method for Discovering and Articulating the DNA

From these interviews, I developed the following crash course method of discovering and articulating the DNA.

- After spending time in prayer and discernment, the pastor initiates the process by drafting his or her mission, vision, and values based on what is deep within the collective hearts and minds of the spiritual leadership in the congregation.

- The pastor asks the key leaders, including the spiritual leaders who have been developed, to spend two weeks individually drafting their own mission, vision, and value statements.

- The pastor and those leaders who completed their assignment gather over a weekend to share and compare their separate drafts, and from these various statements arrive at a prayerful agreement.

- After spending a couple of weeks praying about the newly drafted DNA and if there are no objections, the DNA is shared with a focus group of non-Christians and/or non-members to verify how well the DNA connects with the spiritual hunger of the outside world.

- Next, the statements are shared with the congregation. Small group meetings are set up for dialogue about the DNA for the purpose of refinement and affirmation.

- All of this input is synthesized and presented to the official decision-making group in the church for affirmation. Avoid voting if possible.

- Then, the hard part begins; namely, aligning daily practices with the DNA. This means a number of things: spending money based on the DNA; organizing the congregation around accomplishing the DNA; removing any paid or unpaid leaders who cannot wholeheartedly embrace the DNA; and basing all decisions on the DNA.

The following statements will help you determine if you need to spend time on this unfreezing move or go on to the next one.

❑ Ask any ten of our leaders to recite the Mission of our congregation and you will get the same response almost verbatim.

❑ The mission, vision, and values of our congregation guide every decision our leaders make.

❑ Every piece of paper produced by our church contains the mission statement.

❑ A clear understanding of our mission, vision, and values is part of all leadership training as well as membership training (if you have membership).

❑ The use of our mission, vision, and values to determine what can and can't be done has eliminated most of our decision-making meetings.

❑ People at the lowest level of organization in our church are able to suggest and implement improvements to their own ministry without going through several committees and levels of approval.

❑ Each person in the congregation is free to begin a new ministry without getting permission from a centralized authority as long as it enhances our mission, vision, and values, and two or more other people want to do it with them.

❑ We have in place a process to hold everyone accountable for what they do if it violates the DNA

❑ Our congregation is organized around the mission, vision, and values in such a way that these principles even determine our structure.

❑ We have more of our congregation in ministry than we have serving on boards or committees.

Our average score is:

1 2: Green Light   **3–4:** Yellow Light   **5 or above:** Red Light

Endnotes

1. For more examples, see Mission Statements in the FAQS section of our website http://www.easumbandy.com/
2. Thomas Bandy describes this process a little differently, but the result is the same. He talks about setting the proscriptive boundaries, "those things that a leader may not do rather than what they can do." For more on this, see Thomas G. Bandy, *Christian Chaos* (Nashville: Abingdon Press, 1999).
3. For more on this see Thomas Bandy's books, *Kicking Habits* (Abingdon Press, 1997), and *Christian Chaos* (Nashville: Abingdon Press, 1999).
4. To read the entire stories of the pastors and their congregations, see my work book *Disciple-Making Churches* from EBA at http://www.easumbandy.com/
5. William M. Easum, *The Church Growth Handbook* (Nashville: Abingdon Press, 1990.)

RETIRED PASTOR
PAYING THE MOST
FOR

COIN COLLECTIONS, OLD MAILED ENVELOPES, STAMP COLLECTIONS, & OLD DOCUMENTS

I COME TO YOU

REFERENCES 530-346-7205

CALL JOHN: 530-802-1506

Chapter 7
An Inviting, Growing, and
Sending Community

If you have a solid community that is absent of any ongoing major conflict, and if you have a DNA that is owned and managed by the leadership, you're either just moving into Sphere Three and still may not be reaching out to the outside world, or you are already an innovative congregation that has a history of connecting with the outside world. In either case, it is time to explore how the next four Unfreezing Moves can add to the depth of your life together and your ability to innovate and unleash the congregation. Once again, keep in mind that these unfreezing moves aren't limited to mere linear progression. You may be working on some or all of them at the same time. We have discovered that congregations move into Sphere Three more easily and more effectively when these unfreezing moves build upon and mutually reinforce one another.

Unfreezing Move Three:
Indigenous Worship

1 Corinthians 9:22

Throughout the past one hundred years of Protestant history, worship has consisted of two basic styles, those with order and those with less order; and three basic theologies, liberal, conservative, and fundamentalist. During the first half of the twentieth century, most of the growing edge of Christianity combined order with middle-of-the-road, if not liberal theology. It was common for people to refer to the "order of worship" and then try to merge their theology with their mechanistic (scientific) or formal understanding of human expression while in God's presence.[1] During the latter half of the twentieth century, the growing edge of Christianity began experimenting with a variety of different styles of worship, which appealed to those who have a more conservative, or rather more evangelical, understanding of theology. In both trends, inherited theology and culture had more to do with determining the mission of the congregation than anything else.

The issue today is not contemporary or traditional, liberal or conservative. The issue today is whether or not our worship celebrates the incarnational act of God in Jesus Christ in such a way that people are transformed.

As we enter the third millennium, so far it appears that the majority of the growing segments of Christianity are more concerned with developing an authentic community where people can find acceptance, no matter what worship style or theology undergirds the worship.

What matters today is that the worship is indigenous in the way it carries out the mission of God. Indigenous means that it is in the language, the technology, and the culture of the people that the congregation is trying to reach. To be indigenous means that worship is a relevant, safe place where both Christian and those unconnected to Jesus can have an authentic experience with God.[2] Mission is once again becoming the mother of theology, as it was in the first century. Yet most stuck churches make the style of worship the issue and are willing to split the congregation over the style that is used.

Worship Differences	
Stuck	**Innovative**
Information	Transformation
Doctrine	Experience
Heritage	Community
Reverence	Hope

In most stuck congregations, worship has changed very little the past one hundred years even though the world has undergone radical discontinuity. At the heart of this aging style of worship is information, doctrine, reverence, and heritage. However, Sphere Three congregations base worship on transformation, experience, community, and hope.

The third unfreezing move has to do with changing and/or adding indigenous worship services designed to reach both Christians and those who are unconnected to Jesus in one or more of the following ways:

- Changing the existing worship from slow and reflective, to moving and spirited;

- Adding an additional service with a different style;

- Moving an early morning indigenous service later to 9.30 or 10:00, even if it is at the same time as Sunday School.

Changing worship is usually the most productive of all the unfreezing moves. The easiest way numerically to grow a church and thereby change the system is to begin a worship service with a different style. But be forewarned. It is also the easiest way to start a riot and get run out of the congregation. That is why it is important that the first two unfreezing moves occur first.

Adding an indigenous worship service is often the most productive unfreezing move one can make.

Indigenous worship today has six predominant characteristics around which everything else revolves:

- Worship is moving from an emphasis on choral music toward visualization. The arts are becoming vital to the worship experience once again. More and more, innovative congregations are taking on the characteristics of a gallery that includes great pieces of art from every recorded period in history. Visualization includes art, dramatic vignettes, graphics, and movies. As I am writing this book, Blue Man Group is performing in Las Vegas. Their show is little more than the convergence of visual stunts and rhythmic beat. No words are spoken, but digital words are displayed throughout the performance (www.Blueman.com). I won't be surprised if multiple images take on the same level of importance as music has throughout the century, something like MTV on fast-forward with the sound turned down. In such a format, music becomes the backdrop for the constantly changing images.

- Surround Sound is to today's worship what the pipe organ was to the worship of yesterday. It is not enough to be able to hear the music. Now you literally must be able to feel the beat.

- Technology will support or deliver the entire worship experience. The further we go into the twenty-first century, the more we will realize the effect of the "screen" on worship. Congregations that remain aloof or neutral toward digital technology will not be Sphere Three congregations, even if they are at the moment.

- Participation and interaction from the congregation will be part of the fabric of worship.

- Worship has music that transforms. At the moment, music is still the most important ingredient in an innovative congregation. In most cases I can tell what sphere a congregation is in by simply listening to the music. Of course, there are exceptions such as Church of the Resurrection in Overland Park, Kansas, but even that church is experimenting with modern technology in the traditional services (http://www.cor.org/).

- Above all, worship offers hope and allows people to move beyond contentment to ecstasy.

When I talk about indigenous worship, people in stuck congregations usually respond with the excuse that the cost of such media is too high for them to consider. I respond by asking them question, "Do you have a pipe organ in your church?" The vast majority of dying congregations will answer affirmatively. Then I respond, "What I am talking about will cost much less than a pipe organ. It's just a matter of priorities." Most stuck congregations really wish to remain stuck.

Multiple Tracks

Most congregations will find it hard to survive the next three decades, much less be innovative, without developing multiple tracks of worship: two or more worship services that are very different in style and designed to reach a very different group of people. Different tracks of worship are essential for two reasons: one, the bulk of the people no longer come from Europe, and they require a totally different style of worship; and two, the rapid change of our time has led to a continual change in worship style preferences every few years.

If you're a stuck congregation with one worship service, the odds are high that you need to develop a service with a totally different style, and you might need to add spirit to your traditional service. If you're a Sphere Three congregation that wants to stay that way, you need to experiment with off-the-wall styles of worship to see what will connect with our ever-changing culture.

None of this advice has anything to do with changing or altering the Gospel—though it may get your congregation in touch with the timeless meaning of the Gospel—which is to follow Jesus throughout the world to transform lives. However, the style in which the Gospel is presented must constantly morph into something new. If the style is not influenced by a changing culture, then you are probably not yet offering the Gospel to persons beyond your current reach. Every congregation would do well to have the attitude Paul took with him on his mission to the Gentiles in Athens: "I will do what I have to do in order to rescue some."

Pastors No Longer Merely Preach

Great communicators no longer try to communicate cognitive information or get people to give assent to propositional truths. Instead of hearing or learning about God, people today want to experience the reality behind and beyond the information. The essence of preaching is like a great storyteller exploring some of the great secrets that he or she has learned in life.

Have you seen the new Garth Brooks song?

The time has come when we must experience the convergence of the oral story, the beat of sound, and the visual. Indigenous preaching no longer can be done with three points and poem. Today's audience requires more than just words. As a result, pastors no longer preach an essay. Instead they, along with a team of people, create an experience in which people are transformed by the sum of elements in the experience. The message is still important, but not all-important, as if Protestants are still doing battle as Reformers against the Catholics by emphasizing the Word (exposition on the text of the Scripture) more than the Eucharist (ingestion of Christ's body). That battle is ancient history and it does not matter to those who do not yet follow Jesus. What they want is an experience with the Holy.

	Modern	Bridge	Emerging World
Speaker	Orator	Communicator	Sojourner
Content	Reason	Truth	Experience
Logic	Deductive	Inductive	Loopy
Role	Pious	Professional	Personal
Language	Clear	Music	Visual
Attitude	Efficient	Optimistic	Skeptical
Issues	Faith	God	Jesus

Indigenous Worship Characteristics

Now the entire worship celebration becomes the Message. The message is the convergence of the oral story, the beat of the sound, and visualization of the metaphor. Today's preaching must include the paradox of both/and, the mystery of metaphor and symbol, the open-ended nature of visuals, the complexity of the multi-layered senses, and the pace of a race. If it doesn't, worship will transform neither Christian nor non-Christian.

Pitting contemporary versus traditional worship no longer advances the discussion. Spirited traditional worship is growing churches and making disciples.[3] The key is whether or not the worship is "spirited." Does it have the mystery of the East as well as the high tech of the West? Does it cause the hairs on the back of your neck to stand up? Does it stimulate hearts and challenge minds? Or do we continue to pray that Aunt Suzie does not die during worship while playing the organ?

Creating Indigenous Worship

Indigenous worship, no matter what style, is far more complicated than the type of worship where the worship presenters prepare in isolation, glance at the rulebook, and then it all "sort of comes together" on Sunday morning. Indigenous worship requires the interaction of all eight characteristics (as labeled in the box above), plus clarity about the audience you are trying to reach. Here are the basics of beginning this service.

- Identify your target audience. It is usually best to try to reach one generation younger from the present form of worship. In other words, if all you have at the moment is traditional worship, then reach out to Boomers and offer praise music. If you have praise music, then reach out to the postmodern generations. It is wise not to skip a generation.

- In choosing your music, keep in mind that most people born before 1980 prefer one kind of music and become upset if you offer a variety of music. However, most people born after 1980 enjoy a wide variety of music. This is why I never recommend trying to blend an existing traditional service. You can mix music styles in postmodern worship. Blended worship works adequately in a new service.

• Identify the non-negotiable values and beliefs represented in the new worship experience, and never compromise them for the sake of the experience. Where I see this happening the most is fitting a text to a movie clip that the leader wants to use instead of fitting the movie clip to the text.

• Gather and train a worship design team consisting of at least the following: Worship Team leader, pastor, drama or creative coordinator, graphic or media coordinator, and marketing.

• Gather a music team, including singers and instrumentalists. In time, add writers. Since this seems to be one of the biggest hurdles, here are several tips to finding good musicians.

—Before all else, pray for God to send some musicians your way. Then, put help wanted ads in the local newspapers.

—Place flyers in all the music stores, especially the ones that specialize in rock and roll, and at any local or nearby colleges and community colleges.

—Call the music teachers at the high school and the community college and tell them what you're looking for.

—Find out who's giving guitar lessons in town. They'll know who and where the good musicians are.

—http://www.cmcnet.org/ has a list of bands by city.

—Also, check out "The Almost Definitive Contemporary Christian Music Hot Page" (http://www.afn.org/~mrblue/ccm/ccm.html); Christian Music Online (http://www.cmo.com/); Fair Oaks Learning Center, Fair Oaks Presbyterian Church (http://www.fopc.org/).

- Visit some nearby congregations that you admire and that seem to have indigenous worship in place. Don't worry if the theology matches yours; just observe the methodology.

- Decide on the best time. 9:30 A.M. is still the prime time for reaching Boomers with praise music. There is no one best time to reach postmoderns.

- Gather and train a worship support system consisting of at least the following: prayer hosts, a floor team, and a decision booth.

- Recruit a core group from your congregation to agree to be part of the worship experience for six months. This group should be large enough that the room does not appear to be too empty.

- Preview the service several times before going public.

- Give the service eighteen months to mature before deciding if it is working.

The following statements can aid in determining if your worship is indigenous to the times.

❑ Our worship causes people to experience ecstasy rather than contentment. After every worship service, someone seeks me out to share with me how his or her life was changed during worship.

❑ We spend more time in prayer than in giving announcements.

❑ Our worship focuses on transformation rather than on information.

❑ The majority of the people leave worship hopeful and excited about life.

❑ Our worship service moves rapidly and seldom experiences any unintentional dead spots (a dead spot is more than five seconds where nothing happens).

❑ Our services are filled with the mystery of the East and the technology of the West.

❑ We devote the prime worship hour in our area of the country to those worship services that are best suited to connect with the outside world.

❑ The person responsible for our music will use any kind of music as long as it helps people worship.

❑ We complement the service with visuals.

❑ Our sound system cost more than any other one part of our worship center.

❑ We started a different style of worship service in the last five years.

❑ Our leaders are willing to start a new worship service to connect with new people even if we don't need it due to space limitations.

Our average score is:

1–2: Green Light   **3–4:** Yellow Light   **5 or above:** Red Light

If all you do well is worship with passion, then all you have is a really big show. You must now consider the next Unfreezing Move: Mobilizing the Congregation.

Unfreezing Move Four:
Mobilizing the Congregation for Ministry

Ephesians 4:11–12

When a congregation is free from major ongoing conflict and indigenous worship is in place, it's time to mobilize the congregation for ministry. At least six different systems are found in every effective ministry system where non-ordained, unpaid servants do most of the ministry.

- Identify those who appear ready for discipleship. One equipped paid servant has the capacity to identify up to 125 individuals a year who are ready to be discipled either as a leader or a new disciple. Usually an unpaid servant can identify fewer, simply because of time. This assumes that both paid and unpaid servants don't have to waste time on committees and aren't required to do the pastoral ministry.

- Recruit fifty to seventy-five people who are ready and willing to be coached in their faith development. These people are found within the original group identified. Spend as much time with this group as it takes to determine how open they are to becoming leaders or disciple makers. Encourage those who are not ready to go deeper in their faith by pointing them to one of the growth opportunities that might prepare them.

- Discern who is spiritually ready to go deeper in their faith. Discernment asks, "What gift does this new person bring to the Body that we don't even know that we need?" Delegation asks, "Where does this person fit into our organizational needs?" One focuses on the person and their unique gift and the DNA of the organism, the other focuses on the institutional needs of the machine. The number-one mistake dying churches make is to either allow new people to sit in the pew and vegetate or to swiftly put them on a committee. Most people today do not have the spiritual maturity at this point. They need to be in a Bible study or share group first.

- Equip those who are ready to become disciple makers. Usually paid servants can equip ten to twenty of the original group of individuals into serious, hands-on ministry. Unpaid servants usually can equip and mentor four to ten people. This would normally be the team they have gathered to be part of their ministry.

- Deploy a specific ministry as the next step. Discernment is more important here than delegating. Delegating means that someone gives another a task to perform or responsibility for something that needs to be done. Instead of delegation, disciple makers help people discern for themselves the gift that is within them. People are deployed on the basis of their gift and how they choose to live it out within the mission of the church and the boundaries of the

Value Statement. Discernment is more important than nominations and voting. More and more churches are eliminating most, if not all voting, and relying on God to raise up the leaders and ministries needed.

• Coach the people on your team. Leaders are accessible when needed to help new leaders gain confidence and learn new ministry skills.

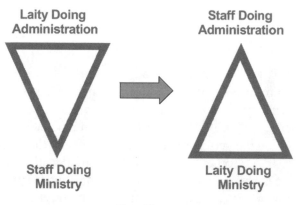

Laity Doing Administration

Staff Doing Administration

Staff Doing Ministry

Laity Doing Ministry

Figure Eleven

The key to understanding lay mobilization is to forget all of the old concepts about volunteers and nominations. Instead of volunteers, think unpaid servants who can be held accountable to the mission of the congregation. Instead of nominations, think of helping people discover their God-given gifts. Instead of Volunteer Coordinators or Directors of Volunteers, think of Mobilizers of Servants or Spiritual Coaches. Instead of thinking about directing or placing volunteers into ministries or committees formed by the institution, think of matching people's God-given gifts, skills, and passion with something they feel God wants them to do and then coaching them to make it happen.

Volunteer Coordinators manage the programmatic needs of the church by recruiting and training anyone who is willing to donate some time or be elected to an office or position. Many or most of the leaders in this process are nominated and elected. Getting people "involved in the church" is usually the goal.

Facilitators of Lay Mobilization design and oversee an organic process based on the DNA of the church and the gifts of called and accountable servants. Little or no nominations and elections are found in this process. This is a movement from doing to being. The purpose is assisting people to grow instead of putting people to work as a means of keeping them tied to the church. The desire is to provide a culture in which people flourish and grow into their potential. The intent has nothing to do with keeping them as members of a local church. Empowerment is usually associated with this model.

> **And the things you have heard me say in the presence of many witnesses entrust to reliable men who will teach others also.**
>
> —2 Timothy 2:2

This kind of mobilization is a movement away from a top-down, centralized organization to a more bottom-up, decentralized organization. In a mobilized congregation, more people are involved in ministry outside the congregation than serve on boards and committees within the congregation. We will come back to organization in the next unfreezing move.

Mobilization of the congregation requires everyone to change their understanding of ministry. (*See* **Figure Eleven**.) For paid servants, the primary paradigm shift is the movement from doing ministry to equipping others to do ministry. Instead of going to work thinking about what one must do, servants go to work dreaming about who they might meet, transform, and mentor. Instead of trying to get a ministry done or a task performed, servants look for new people to mentor, equip, and send out into ministry. The shift is from doing to finding. For unpaid servants, the primary shift is from sitting in the pews or going to committees to being responsible for accomplishing all that occurs within and outside of the congregation. Unpaid servants are no longer Doers who do the will of the Deciders. They are now both Deciders and Doers.[4]

Leadership Multiplication

To mobilize a congregation, leaders must think multiplication rather than addition. The best method of mobilizing a congregation I have seen is what Wayne Cordeiro, pastor of New Hope Christian Fellowship, calls Fractaling (http://www.newhope-hawaii.org/). I used a similar method in the late 80's to staff the congregation I pastored and I called it the Hub System. Its origins come from both Exodus 18 and from the way in which Jesus trained his disciples.

Fractaling is the constant repetition of leadership over and over. It is everyone training everyone to be a leader. Every leader asks, who can I get to help me on this mission? and how can I break this project down into small enough pieces to include lots of people in the mission? So, how does fractaling work?

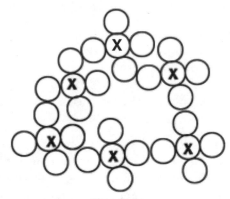

Figure Twelve

The key to fractaling is to make sure that the original fractal for the whole church is done properly. It must include the DNA of the congregation in macrocosm. From there everything else fractals out. For example, the four fractals of the Hub System at the church I pastored were: Worship (Invite), Administration, Lay Ministry (Grow), and Outreach (Send).

For our discussion, lets assume that all fractals are in multiples of four. (*See* **Figure Twelve**.) Let's also assume that our task is to add staff for the purpose of creating a new indigenous service of worship. We go looking for someone to be the worship leader and gather a team who will be responsible for the new worship. This person's mission is not to do worship but to gather and equip a team of four people who will help by finding four other people who will find four other people and so on. Here is how that person would proceed.

The worship leader must first determine the basic four pieces of indigenous worship for your particular setting. For example, the worship leader may decide these four are Singers, Instruments, Logistics, and Visuals. The worship leader then identifies, recruits, and equips a person to take responsibility for each of the four. Each of these four will identify, recruit, and equip four people to make a team for their area. As the congregation grows, each of these teams will fractal several times. For example, the logistics team might fractal by dividing responsibilities into nursery, ushers, hosts, and decision table. Or the instruments might fractal into keyboards, drums, pianos, and organs. What started out as a small team of five people has now escalated into numerous teams.

Here are some keys to multiplying leaders:

- Pastors understand that their primary fractal or hub is their flock rather than the whole congregation, and they spend most of their time with them.

- No one is responsible for more than four people plus their spouses, so every ten people have a shepherd (spouses are included).

- Instead of asking a few people to do a lot, ask a lot of people to do only what they love doing and hold them accountable.

- Focus the amount of time people have to spend in ministry on those things that they are gifted to do. This way no one burns out.

The following statements will help you determine if this is the unfreezing move with which you should begin.

❏ We have more people in hands-on ministry outside of our congregation than we do working within the congregation.

❏ We have more servants than volunteers.

❏ We never invite people to serve the church, instead we encourage them to discover what God has created them to do best with their life and assist them in doing it.

❏ Our leaders understand that one of their primary callings is to raise up and equip more leaders.

❏ Except for the amount of time spent, we expect the same level of dedication from our unpaid servants as we do from those who are paid.

❏ We realize that any form of service is the same in God's sight and should be in ours.

❏ We encourage people to continue in their chosen area of ministry as long as it rejuvenates their spiritual life and enhances the mission, vision, and values of the congregation.

❏ Our key leaders spend more time in coaching other leaders than in doing hands-on ministry.

❏ Our paid servants seldom visit the hospitals, offer funerals, or weddings.

❏ The unpaid servants who have a major role in leading someone to Christ play a major role in that person's baptism.

❏ Our unpaid servants take communion to our shut-ins.

Our average score is:

1–2: Green Light   **3–4:** Yellow Light   **5 or above:** Red Light

Unfreezing Move Five: Redemptive Missional Opportunities

1 Corinthians 9:22

We are now at the heart of what it means to be the Church of Jesus Christ. Redemptive missional opportunities are the reason the Church exists. Everything Sphere Three and Four congregations do is focused on redemptive missional opportunities.

Sphere One & Two	Sphere Three & Four
Mission Committee	Missional Attitude
Active	Discipled
Program	Reason for Being
Service	Redemption
Raising Money	Sending People

Sphere One and Two congregations attempt to get new people involved in the organizational and/or programmatic life of the congregation whether or not they have any biblical and spiritual foundation from which to minister. Their goal is to involve people as quickly as possible so they won't leave the church. The result is that most people are never discipled. Placing people into serving roles before being discipled usually results in a congregation of biblically and spiritually illiterate—good people doing good works with no idea of how to use these missional opportunities in a redemptive way.

Sphere One and Two congregations don't seem to worry about redemptive results because they think of outreach ministries as services to the community rather than redemptive opportunities. We see this demonstrated often in weekday pre-school or daycare ministries. These congregations do nothing to intentionally connect spiritually with the participating families. Often these ministries function as separate entities from the church with little or no contact between the school and congregation other than financial. In many cases, the lay leaders of these congregations even see these potential ministries as intrusions and imposition upon their use of the church facilities.

Sphere One and Two congregations usually have a Missions Committee and perceive missions as various programs or services offered by the congregation to people outside their congregation, usually some other country, or at least across town. Their role is to raise money to send somewhere so someone else can do the redemptive part.

On the other hand, Sphere Three and Four congregations find little reason to have a Missions Committee. They don't need one because everything they do is missional. They are redemptive outposts on a mission field. They realize that the entire world is a mission field, especially their backyard. Their goal is to transform their community and world, not serve the community. They want the actions of their people to be redemptive and transformational, and not just "doing good."

As a result, these congregations seek to evaluate where new people are in their spiritual journey before asking them to serve, especially in any leadership capacity. They want them to have a faith they can share while serving the outside world. Churches are not service organizations. Everything a congregation does should have something to do with bringing the Good News to bear on the lives of unreached people.

Attitude Is the Key

At the heart of redemptive missional opportunities lies an attitude and passion that is sensitive to those who are unconnected to Jesus. Nurturing a passion for and sensitivity to unconnected individuals is the key to this unfreezing move. You began this part of the transformation in the very first unfreezing move when you began to develop a cadre of spiritual giants. If you are not succeeding in the first unfreezing move, it will be impossible for your leaders to grasp the importance of this unfreezing move. They may say they want the church to grow, but what they mean is they want more people so that it will be easier to reach the budget. Or they may feel as if the church should be active in the community, but see little difference in what Christians do and what is accomplished by the Lions or Rotarians. Sphere One and Two congregations seldom understand that the very soul of their congregation is at stake in this unfreezing move. To fail to connect with unconnected persons in your area of the world is to fail to be the church and to become a hospice or hospital—but not a church. Sphere Three and Four congregations exist to send their newly discipled servants out into the mission field with Jesus to transform both the people and the culture.

The Result of Passion

Most effective redemptive missional opportunities begin because someone's heart burns to see that particular mission happen. Sphere One and Two congregations often try to brainstorm ideas for new mission programs or projects that will serve the community and maybe bring in some new members. Then they try to find some people to carry it out. Sphere Three and Four congregations allow these missional opportunities to bubble up out of the passion of individual servants instead of trying to manufacture them in some centralized back room.

The following statements will help you determine if this is where to begin the unfreezing move.

❑ We evaluate personal spiritual development before placing persons into a ministry.

❑ Most of our ministries focus either on reaching the unreached or growing those who participate in our congregation deeper in their faith.

❑ We believe and encourage every person in our congregation to join Jesus on the mission field.

❑ The amount of leadership people can attain depends on the depth of their spiritual life and their commitment to joining Jesus on the mission field.

❑ We will add a new ministry or terminate an existing one even if it has a long tradition in order to ensure that everything we do has a redemptive emphasis.

❑ All of our social ministries have a redemptive component to them.

Our average score is:

1–2: Green Light   **3–4:** Yellow Light   **5 or above:** Red Light

Unfreezing Move Six:
Organizing Around the DNA

At some point in the transition from Sphere One to Sphere Three, effective congregations discover that they are not organized to carry out their DNA and that their organizational structure has become a major roadblock to ministry. When this tension becomes evident, they need to restructure. This restructuring can be done all at once or in stages. Most of the time it is done in stages—non-working committees are intentionally left unchaired, new ad-hoc teams are started, boards are reduced in size, and so on.

> **Restructuring never solves a problem. All it does is to facilitate the forward progress of an already effective congregation.**

The church where I served Christ for twenty-four years had been allowing the needs of our mission to slowly cause us to change our structure for more than a decade by dropping, adding, and rearranging pieces of the system. However, at one point in the development of our small group system we began to hear people say, "I would love to lead a small group, but I'm too busy." When we would inquire about their busyness, we learned that they were engaged in several activities and committees within the church, none of them as important as leading a small group. When we asked them if they would lead a small group if they were relieved from their commitment to all of the church activities and committees, they almost unanimously said yes. We knew at this point that it was time to finish dismantling our outdated structure, which had been imposed upon us by our denomination. Doing so was illegal at the time, but it was necessary for innovation to go forward. When we began talking about restructuring, most of the leadership understood the reason. Also, a decade later, my denomination saw fit to change its rules almost identically to what we had done earlier.

The same results happen in a congregation. Often beginning the process of restructuring is as simple as one key leader changing his or her habits. When a key leader changes habits, the whole system either shifts to accommodate the new action, or the leader is asked to leave. The story of Dick Wills, pastor of Christ UMC in Ft. Lauderdale, is a testimony to how powerful it can be for the leader to radically change his or her behavior. You can read his story in his book, *Waking to God's Dream*.[5]

Sphere One congregations are seldom successful when they try to begin their transformation from Sphere One to Sphere Two by restructuring. About the only time this works is when the congregation is about to close or has been closed and is being restarted. Otherwise, attempting to restructure too early in the movement from Sphere One to Sphere Three can be counterproductive for two reasons: since the old guard doesn't like change, too much of the leader's energy is diverted from raising up spiritual leaders to convincing and/or placating the old guard; and not enough solid ministry is in place yet to warrant the time spent restructuring. At least get the DNA in place first and develop a cadre a new leaders before attempting to restructure.

Someone once asked me why The Church of Latter Day Saints was growing so fast. My answer was swift: "They're organized to grow. Everything they do is designed to produce more Mormons." The key to restructuring is the old adage "form follows function." The mission of the congregation should determine how the congregation is organized. This means that no one organizational system will work for all congregations even if they are in the same denomination.

The following statements will aid you in deciding if this unfreezing move is the place to begin.

❑ We never refer to *Robert's Rules of Order* and we seldom refer to any Constitution, Policy Statement, or denominational rule book.

❑ We strive to keep our structure as simple as possible and avoid multiple forms of checks and balances.

❑ If we have to choose between putting someone on a committee (if we have any) and sending them into the mission field with Jesus, we always choose the mission field.

❑ Major new ministries can begin within sixty days.

❑ Very few unpaid servants are involved in the day-to-day operations of the congregation.

❑ All of our outreach ministries are designed to connect with the unreached and none of them are seen merely as services to the community.

Our average score is:

1–2: Green Light   **3–4:** Yellow Light   **5 or above:** Red Light

---

1. The most notable exceptions to this generalization were Southern Baptists, Pentecostals (Assemblies of God), and Missionary Alliance.
2. For more on indigenous worship, see the chapter in *Growing Spiritual Redwoods* (Nashville, Abingdon Press, 1996).
3. One of the best examples of this is Church of the Resurrection UMC in Kansas City, Kansas. Go to www.cor.org.
4. For more on this shift in attitude see my book *Leadership on the OtherSide* (Nashville: Abingdon Press, 2000)
5. Dick Wills, *Waking To God's Dream* (Nashville: Abingdon Press, 1999).

Chapter 8
Staffing for the Mission Field

1 Timothy 5:17-18

A congregation's most important assets are the gifts, skills, and passion quotient of the paid and unpaid servants (staff). How a church staffs, and what it expects its servants (staff) to accomplish is essential to joining Jesus on the mission field. A mistake here throws out of balance everything else the congregation attempts.

Staff is defined in this chapter as both paid and unpaid servants. Both paid and unpaid servants are held accountable to the same standards. The only exception is the amount of time committed by both, and as we will see in moment, even the amount of time committed can be the same. So, I'll use the words staff and servants interchangeably.

Unfreezing Move Seven:
Hire Servants, Not Professionals

Ephesians 4:11-12

The three most dramatic changes to occur the past twenty years in staffing Sphere Three and Four congregations are:

- The shift from professional paid staff who direct volunteers in carrying out programs to paid servants who equip and coach unpaid servants to carry out most of the pastoral responsibilities.

- The shift from using all paid staff to using combinations of paid and unpaid servants to fill a role or using unpaid servants in the place of paid staff.

- The shift from the lead pastor seeing the entire congregation as her or his flock to seeing a few key staff positions as his or her flock.

• The shift from the charismatic, lone-ranger type of leadership to more of a team-based approach to ministry.

In Sphere Three and Four congregations, the primary role of paid servants is to create an environment in which leaders, at every level, are equipped and encouraged to replicate the DNA of the church through living out their spiritual gifts. As we learned earlier, paid servants are never hired to do ministry. Instead, they gather and equip teams of unpaid servants for both pastoral and mission ministry.

What do we want our paid and unpaid servants to do: equip the saints to be with Jesus on the mission field or take care of our members?

Leaders in Sphere One and Two congregations find these changes extremely hard to comprehend, much less attempt. They have become so accustomed to being cared for by professionals that they find it impossible to comprehend the biblical truth about how congregations as suppose to function (See Ephesians 4:11-12). This inability to comprehend and make the necessary changes is a critical flaw in these congregations. It shows their self-centeredness instead of their passion to join Jesus on the mission field.

Stuck congregations wishing to move to Sphere Three need to determine what their priority is: whether they want their paid servants to take care of their membership first, and then, if there is time, increase church membership; or whether they want them to develop disciples who will serve with Jesus on the mission field. For most of the last fifty years, church leaders have expected professional staff to take good care of the membership first, and if there is time left, increase the membership roles of the church. Sooner or later such a decision is fatal because it is the exact opposite of what we see Jesus doing during his ministry. God simply will not honor those congregations.

Sphere Three and Four congregations expect the efforts of paid and unpaid servants to result in transformed people who later become so equipped that they can take care of others instead of being cared for by church professionals. These congregations are moving away from the ordained, professional, generalist who cared for the flock and represented the congregation in the community, and are equipping paid and unpaid servants to specialize around their gifts and skills to enhance the mission of the congregation. The rapidly changing climate of our culture has opened the door to the acceptance of a wide variety of different forms of staffing, such as part-time, homegrown, nonprofessionals; bi-vocational leaders and pastors; team-based leadership; and outsourced consultants. Many of these forms of staffing more closely resemble the leadership of the first-century congregation. Such widespread acceptance of these various forms of staffing among Sphere Three and Four congregations will lead to the emergence of many new forms of non-conventional congregations. This trend will continue and will add fuel to ministries like house churches, the numerous non-denominational new church starts, storefront congregations, café churches, cyber churches, biker churches, and the continued downsizing of the postmodern congregation, and perhaps fewer mega-churches. Unfortunately Sphere One and Two congregations continue to cling to the professional model of ordained clergy.

Throughout this chapter keep in mind that any committed person can be considered staff even if she or he is not paid. We are seeing more and more laity (I've avoided using that word so far but can't find a way to avoid it here) who have made it financially in life devote themselves full-time to the ministry of their congregation without any payment.[1]

The Basic Staff Roles

In congregations that can afford it, the roles described in this section are normally paid. However, small, new, and non-conventional congregations should keep in mind that these are descriptions of the key staff roles that a congregation needs filled first, and that they can be filled by unpaid servants. So, a lack of money is never an issue when it comes to staffing, even for the smaller congregations. Any size congregation can accomplish equipping leaders for ministry, if the leadership desires and encourages it.

For the past five decades congregations that could afford it, staffed themselves with a full-time pastor who cared for the congregation and participated in the local service organization and council of churches; a part-time or full-time Youth Director who kept the youth busy with programs and out-of-town mission projects; a part-time Music Director whose function was to prepare the choir to sing on Sunday and perhaps do a musical once or twice a year; a part-time or full-time secretary who did the bulletin, answered the phone, and gossiped with the long-term members. The next person added was usually a part-time or full-time Education Director who was responsible primarily for Sunday school and perhaps Vacation Bible School. Today, this formula is fatal. Yet, sadly it is still used or aspired to by many Sphere One and Two congregations.

The basic servants in Sphere Three and Four congregations of the twenty-first century have a much different configuration and expectation. Their basic servants consist of the equivalent of a full-time:

- Lead pastor, whose primary responsibility is to guard the DNA, hire and equip paid servants, and insure that people are being equipped to join Jesus on the backyard mission field.

- Worship leader (Inviting), who may or may not read music and who is responsible for gathering and equipping a team to be responsible for the entire worship experience, including the music, graphics, lighting, sound, drama, arts, and so forth.

- Lay mobilizer (Growing), who designs and oversees a process that insures that everyone from the parking lot to the mission field is welcomed and grown into spiritual giants who exercise their gifts.

- Administrator, who insures that everything and everyone in the support team undergirds and makes it easier and more productive for the unpaid and paid servants to join Jesus on the mission field.

- Outpost leader (Sending), whose role is to understand and

interpret the culture of the mission field to the paid and unpaid staff and to insure that every ministry of the congregation has a backyard mission component to it.

The Five Most Important Staff
Lead Pastor
Worship Leader
Lay Mobilizer
Administrator
Outpost Leader

Beyond these five basic roles, the remaining servants depend on the particular, unique mission of the congregation.

A debate is underway today over the order in which congregations should add paid or unpaid staff. Some are now saying that the role of the administrator is the second position to fill. I don't agree. I have taught for some time that the first paid position (after obtaining a lead pastor) a congregation should add is the worship leader. I still feel this way because in order for worship to transform people it has to be a total experience of word, sound, and image. The role of the worship leader is as important as that of the lead pastor. If the congregation has a full-time pastor, then the first addition should be the equivalent of a full-time worship leader, and so on, as I have outlined the roles above.

You may have noticed that when describing the staff of Sphere Three and Four congregations I did not say full- or part-time, but "the equivalent of full-time." Sphere Three and Four congregations function more around teams of people than Sphere One or Two congregations and often put one or more part-time people together to fill one position. However, like many smaller congregations, they also use many unpaid servants to fill the roles that are normally filled by paid staff. The basic roles can be filled with a single full-time person or by a combination of people, each one bringing a different gift to the team.

Ratio of Staff to Worship

There is a direct correlation between the numbers of unpaid servants on the mission field and the number of paid servants (staff) who equip the congregation for mission. Sphere One and Two congregations might understand this statement better if it read, "There is a direct correlation between the number of volunteers and the number of paid staff." The more paid staff there are that equip, the more unpaid servants (volunteers) there will be. If paid staff equip other leaders, then the number of leaders in a congregation grows, and paid staff never takes the place of unpaid servants.

In a Sphere Three or Four congregation, the ratio of staff to worship attendance can be as high as one staff person to every two hundred to two hundred and fifty people in worship. It all depends on the number of unpaid servants who function like paid staff. In a Sphere One or Two congregation attempting to make the transformation into Sphere Three, the ratio is much lower: one staff person to every one hundred people in worship, because of the difficulty of transformation. Remember: Staff can be paid or unpaid. Caution: When figuring up your ratio of staff to worship attendance, do not count unpaid staff in the equation unless they are held to the same standards as the paid servants.

How Staff Relate to the Congregation

Sphere One and Two congregations expect staff to be responsible for everyone in the congregation. This is especially true of the pastor who is expected to be the shepherd of the entire congregation and to be personally responsible for the spiritual well-being of everyone, including the shut-ins. However, Sphere Three and Four congregations allow their staff to focus on a much smaller group of people. They've discovered that the fewer persons there are to be supervised (paid and unpaid servants), the more productive the team. I discovered years ago that four is the best number to supervise and configured our staff accordingly. The pastor is shepherd of the staff and often this staff consists only of the four basic positions mentioned below. (*See* **Figure Thirteen**.) The pastor is responsible

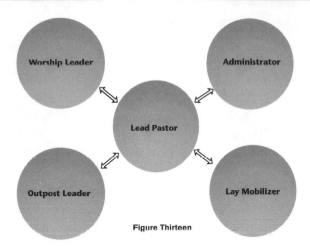

Figure Thirteen

for the spiritual well-being of those four people, plus any spouses. Each of those four are responsible for the key four people in their area of ministry, and so forth.

If you are going to staff a congregation, use the example shown in Figure Thirteen. These are the primary staff that you should spend time equipping and pastoring, plus any spouses. Expect them to do the same with four key people in their area of ministry, and so forth. This ensures that no one burns out and that everyone has time to be involved in continual personal growth.

Bringing Together a Staff Team

Bringing together a team of paid and unpaid servants is one of the most challenging and important decisions a congregation ever makes. It is so important that the only people who should be involved in the decision are the ones who are directly affected by the decision. In the case of securing the four key positions in Figure Ten, it is best if only the lead pastor is involved because the relationship between these five persons is crucial to all else that happens in the congregation. Get this team right, and the probability of the DNA being embedded throughout all of the staff is much greater.

Some groups demand that the congregation have some form of personnel committee to hire, terminate, and supervise paid staff. I don't agree. If a personnel committee exists, it should only work with the lead pastor. They supervise him or her, and the lead pastor or executive pastor hires, terminates, and supervises the key team leaders, who also hire, terminate, and supervise their teams, and so on. The only way to develop a team environment is if the teams have the freedom to be responsible for the competency and growth of their team members. It is total nonsense for a group of people who don't spend most of their time working in the ministry of the congregation to have the ability to hire, fire, and terminate staff about whose job functions they may know little.

Whether you are hiring a paid person or choosing an unpaid person to fill a key role, the following process will help assure you of finding the right people. Before having a personal interview with the person you are considering, make sure that you know as much as you can about her or his character, personality, and spiritual passion or gifts. This is relatively easy to achieve when bringing people on board from within the congregation. If you are looking outside the congregation, before spending the money to bring a person to the church for an interview, have the candidates:

- Submit a resume of where they have served, along with three references.

- Take several personal inventories to see if they have the temperament and gifts that are needed to be on your team. These inventories do not measure the skills of the person but provide hints about how this person might use his or her gifts on your team and how you might better equip her or him. Many inventories exist to assist you in this process.[2]

- If the candidates are at a distance, contact them by phone and narrow the choice to one to three candidates to be brought to the church for personal interviews.

- Do not be afraid to spend some time and money before you do an interview. In the long run, it will save you money as well as pain.

The following process for on-site interviewing consists of four questions that are asked of the candidates by the senior pastor or team leader at the beginning of the interview process. The questions are sequential, with each one built on the one before it. The interviewer proceeds to the next question only if the candidate enthusiastically and adequately responds to the previous question. If not, the interview is terminated without wasting any more of the candidate's or the church's time. Here are the questions:

- "Describe for me your spiritual journey." More important than one's skills or talents, attributes or qualities, is whether or not the person is on a spiritual journey and has a personal story to tell. What you want are people who passionately yearn to pursue their spiritual journey as well as the journey of others. Look for people who excite you just by telling their story. If they don't excite you, they won't excite anyone else.

- "How do you feel about our DNA?" Hand the person a copy of your Mission, Vision, and Values and look into their eyes as they read the document. Do their eyes dance and sparkle as they read it? Are you convinced the person resonates with the DNA? Does his or her response convince you that this person would be a great ambassador for your congregation's DNA? You are looking for staff that is so in love with your DNA that they are willing to set aside personal agendas and conduct their ministry based on what is best for the congregation.

- Avoid giving the candidate a job description. You want to recruit people around your DNA, not a job or task to perform. You're asking this person to take a journey where perhaps neither of you has gone before, and therefore a map must be drawn as you go. Job descriptions are the prelude to hearing staff say, "That's not my job."

If you feel you must have a job description, then have it read something like this:

- "Your mission is to use your gifts and skills to enhance the mission of (name of your church) by raising up and equipping (place a number here) new leaders each year who will join Jesus on the mission field."

- "What gifts do you bring that would add value to our DNA?" Instead of asking the candidate to do something that the church feels it needs done, let the candidate explain to you how he or she would use his or her gifts to enhance the DNA. Doing this helps insure that the person understands how his or her particular gifts bring more completeness to the DNA. If the answer excites you, continue the interview.

- "How would you go about adding this value?" Using this approach allows the Holy Spirit to work more freely in your midst. You may be surprised how often this approach leads to effective ministries that would otherwise never be discovered. It might be good at this point to explore if the candidate has any previous experience working in a team-based environment. Listen for such responses as: "I know I'll need to put together a team because I don't have all the necessary skills to do the kind of ministry that the culture calls for, but I'm open to learning them;" or "To be effective here, I'll have to develop and empower a team." Such responses are what you want to encourage in all leaders.

The appropriate paid staff with whom they will be working interviews those who make it to the end of the interview process. Have as many appropriate paid and unpaid staff as possible to interview the candidate. Start the interview at 8:00 AM, with the lead pastor or team leader asking the above questions. Then at thirty-minute intervals, have the paid staff individually interview the candidate and ask questions based on their role within the team. Give each of them a sheet of paper that asks two things: Would you hire this person? If yes, what further questions would you like asked of this person? If no, why? At the end of the interview process, the lead pastor or team leader tallies the interviews and lists the questions. If any one of the interviewers votes not to hire, do not hire this person.

Depending on the size of the church, this process could take several days. At the end of the process, the lead pastor or team leader would meet again with the candidate. Part of the purpose of a grueling schedule is to see how the person's stamina holds out. Don't bring anyone on board who has low energy. If the candidate did not pass the interview process, the lead pastor or team leader should explain why. The candidate then learns from the experience and perhaps some other congregation is helped in the future.

If you are ready to offer the candidate an invitation to join the staff team, have her or him go back home and design her or his own job description. Then have the candidate return and negotiate the details together. This way insures that the candidate understands the mission and has an essential part in designing his or her work.

The Most Common Staffing Mistakes

The most common mistakes I see congregations make in regard to staffing are:

- Hiring a paid servant even when in doubt because the job needs filling. It is better to do without staff than to hire or appoint someone whom you will have to let go in a short time.

- Assigning your best people to fix problems. Put your best people on the most important positive opportunities.

- Putting off terminating a paid servant even though you know you need to let him or her go. Cut your losses as soon as possible. Even unqualified paid servants build relationships within the congregation. The longer they stay, the more relationships they develop, and when you finally let them go more people are hurt.

- Having someone on the staff who is a mission rather than on a mission. Many Sphere One and Two congregations have long-term staff, especially in the office, who can no longer function well but they keep them because they are "family." As a result, the mission suffers. Instead of keeping them as staff, either let them go or move their salary to the mission budget and hire someone to fill their role. The kind thing is to help them find a place where they can fill a needed role in the mission.

• Hiring people based on credentials rather than on their particular gifts or skills.

• Hiring associate pastors who are generalists rather than specialists who are usually not ordained. Most associates never stay long enough to be of any value (you lose the first year and the last year of most staff) and want to do the same things as the lead pastor. In many traditions they cost at least twice as much as non-ordained people.

The following statements will assist you in determining if this is the unfreezing move on which you need to focus.

❑ Our paid and unpaid staff constantly share their vision with everyone around them.

❑ The primary role of our paid and unpaid servants is to equip the congregation to do the pastoral ministry and to be on the mission field with Jesus.

❑ No one on our staff is stretched so thin that he or she is about to burn out.

❑ All of our staff is provided enough continuing education funds to attend two three-day conferences away each year.

❑ We have a consistent and thorough screening process for hiring new staff that takes at least an entire day and the completion of at least one personal inventory.

❑ All of our paid servants, including our worship leader/music director, custodians, and secretaries, either have a passion for or are supportive of the congregation's mission to make disciples.

❑ Our ratio of staff to the average worship service equals the above-suggested ratios.

❑ Many of our key staff have never been to seminary.

Our average score is:

1–2: Green Light   **3–4:** Yellow Light   **5 or above:** Red Light

---

1. Before I left the local church in 1993 to become a consultant, we had two full-time, non-paid servants working on our staff in addition to the paid servants.
2. The Myers-Briggs inventory is one of the most widely used personal inventories. Here is a list of other available inventories:
   - DISC, Contact Jim Beard at NAMS, 800-441-6267, $50 each.
   - Role Preference Inventory (self scoring): 800-443-1976, $5 each.
   - The most complete spiritual gift inventory is *Networking*, from Zondervan.
   - Some congregations may want to use the Easum Inventory because of its thoroughness, user friendliness, long-term applicability, and low cost.
   - The Birkman Method (713-623-2760) and the inventory prepared by Gallup (Ask for Rosanne Liesveld, 301 S. 68th St. Pl. Lincoln, NE 68510, 402-489-9000; http://education.gallup.com/info/strengthsFinder.asp) are two of the most thorough inventories. The benefits are many—especially the ability to talk with a consultant about the scores. It will tell you how to respond to this person in ways that assure the person has the best opportunity to reach his or her potential.

Chapter 9
Getting the Most Out of
Your Property

Exodus 40:34–38

At the stroke of midnight 1997, a famous casino was imploded to make way for a casino more in tune with the technology of our times. What made this event so interesting was that the old casino was less than ten years old. As I watched the casino fall in on itself, all I could think was "What if Christians loved their mission as much as the casino owners loved making money? What would happen to most of our church facilities?" You know the answer: Most of them would be imploded.

During the twentieth century, property and place were of extreme importance. Many people grew up and died in the same home or town and sat in the same sanctuary most, if not all, of their lives. As a result, many long-term members would just as soon see their church close rather than relocate it. New church pastors have told me more than once that they are tired of their leaders pushing them to buy property and build a sanctuary so that finally they can be a "real church." The sanctuary was considered by many to be "God's House" and was considered sacred space. The "field of dreams" mindset was dominant. It was called, somewhat facetiously, the "edifice complex" even in the 1970's. Erect a new building, and people came no matter what went on inside. It was the thing to do. Some leaders in Sphere One and Two congregations actually believed that one way to help people become more connected to their church was to have a building program!

> **Many church leaders believe that the twenty-first century will be more like the first century than the twentieth century. If this is so, then Christianity's understanding of property will undergo profound change.**

So when it comes to "church property," feelings run deep. When people say, "I love my church," they are referring as much to the actual facility as they are expressing the relationships that they have built up in that facility over the years. Otherwise, why is it normal for Sphere One and Two congregations to spend more time, energy, and money on the upkeep of their facilities than on everything else combined? Why else would a congregation that burned down rebuild the exact same facility on the same piece of property that is located in a commercial zone where no one lives anymore and has no room for parking? Instead, they could have sold the valuable piece of property (now commercial), moved to a new location, and had money left over. Sphere One and Two congregations usually love their facilities more than their God. They should heed the paraphrase of the first commandment: "Thou shalt not love thy buildings (literally, idols) more than thy God."

However, vast migrations throughout the world are underway and have been for many years. More people move around the country than stay put in one place. People are constantly changing churches. Postmodernism has put an end to the concept of sacred space. Cyberspace is redefining our sense of place. Property is less the house a person owns and more the things a person collects. The "field of dreams" mindset works only if something good is already happening in the life of a congregation.[1] What property was to the twentieth century, mission and community will be to the twenty-first century. That spells trouble for most of the traditional ways of approaching church property.

Property has not been important to transformational leadership until recently. Now, because of the rapid changes in society and the constant movement of people, how congregations use their property is becoming one of the issues that sets the innovative congregation apart from the rest. Sphere Three and Four congregations look on property as little more than a means to an end. If the property no longer supports the ministry, then redo or change the property. Property is looked upon the same way the Israelites looked upon the Ark of the Covenant—it is something to be picked up and moved to wherever God is leading you. The twenty-first century congregation is becoming mobile again.

Unfreezing Move Eight:
Space and Place as Metaphor

The Disney people have shown the world the importance of understanding space and place as metaphor. From the parking lot to the rides to the way they have you sign your credit card, everything is designed for the customer to have a total experience in fantasy. Disney knows that the context sets the stage for the experience. Does your congregation understand the importance of setting? Do your facilities say to persons driving by, "Hey, we understand your world and if you come inside we will treat you with the same tender loving care that you see on the outside driving by." Where we meet and what our facilities look like betray our understanding of the world around us.

Consider the following examples of space and place as metaphor:

- To build today in the Western world without taking into account the importance of visuals and sound is like ignoring the technological revolution of the last thirty years. Do we really believe that postmodern people won't notice and be turned off from the start?

- To choose to worship in a storefront may be more a statement of mission than a lack of money. Consider the new church plant in Atlanta, Georgia, called The Cell (http://www.thecellonline.com). They have an outright disdain for owning property and are making an attempt at never being landed gentry or taking down any trees in order to pave a parking lot. The Cell utilizes homes, bars, restaurants, and even a tattoo parlor. Instead of having an inanimate object present an image to the community (i.e. a building, playground, etc.), they feel that using the animate objects of people to represent the community of faith is more effective. For a list of congregations using this method, go to http://www.easumbandy.com/FAQS/renting_space.htm.

- To hold worship in a bar may be a statement that the church is willing to meet the unreached on their turf. New Life

133

Christian Church in Centreville, Virginia (http://newlifenet.org/) has a ministry targeting young adults that meets Sunday nights at the Shark Club, a local bar. The Church sees it as a major outreach to minister to the unconnected. "It's the only church service where you have to be twenty-one to enter." The service is called "The Well."

• To meet in a café is one way to say to the world that you understand the importance of getting an extra-hot-triple-tall-skim-latte. Café churches seem to be a trend among those churches reaching young adults, just as coffee houses attracted Boomers to youth ministries in the early 1970's. CentrePointe church (http://www.stainedglass.com/centre-pointe) tries to create the feel of a coffee house.

To use art extensively throughout a facility is an attempt to acknowledge the growing place that art plays in the postmodern world, as well as a way to reach the art community. Thirteen-year-old congregation (as of 2001) Westwinds Community Church in Jackson, Missouri, (http://www.westwinds.org/) is an excellent example of using a facility as a metaphor. The facility is highly artistic in almost every way. They use art pieces, large tactile visuals, media, drama, music, scent, seating configuration, and lighting to create an experiential environment designed to increase the incidence of people "bumping into the presence of God."

Place and space are metaphors that speak volumes. So the next time you are tempted to allow the church grass to grow tall or to let the paint on the sign out front peel or to have outdated dates and themes, remember that it says to those passing by, "This is the way we will treat you if you come inside."

Innovative Options for Existing Congregations

Sphere Three and Four congregations always look for ways to reach out to the world beyond, even when their facilities are stretched. That is the way God designed the Church.

For Congregations With Inadequate Facilities

The vast majority of congregations in North America don't have facilities adequate for postmodern ministry. Either they have a poor sound system; a stained glass window where a rear projection screen should be; too many stairs for the elderly and parents with infants; long, dark, narrow hallways that discourage conversation; a long, narrow sanctuary; or not enough space for parking. Like the ten-year-old casino, some of these congregations need to come down or do something, even if it is wrong.

My fear is that the majority of Sphere One and Two congregations will do one of the following: 1) Continue to do nothing and die. I find it interesting that many church leaders in Sphere One and Two truly believe that they can continue doing nothing different and things will get better. (See http://education.gallup.com.) 2) Remodel and die. Many church leaders are driven more by sentiment and heritage than mission. 3) Add ramps and an elevator and die. This is yet another example of self-centeredness.

Here are some solid options for congregations with inadequate facilities:

- Begin a new congregation in the area, and prepare for the closing of the mother church. We don't see this happening often because of the parochial attitudes of the original congregation.

- Sell the property to an indigenous ministry and move out. We constantly hear denominational officials voice their disdain for this option because they want to continue a denominational presence in that part of town. It amazes me that they would want to continue the kind of presence that a dying, decaying, isolated, and totally unfriendly congregation gives to the community.

- Develop a new direction of ministry designed to reach out to the area, while at the same time making the building accessible to all ages. Obviously, this option offers some hope to both those who have kept the church open over the years and the unreached in the area. One of the most recent and best examples of this is St. John's UMC in downtown Houston, Texas. The church was going to be closed by the denomination when one of the pastors of that same denomination asked if he could have a chance to rejuvenate the congregation. In two years the congregation went from seven people in worship to over 3500 because an unordained couple, sent by the pastor from his church to St. John's, took the ministry into the streets and began serving meals to the homeless both outside the church and in the sanctuary.

- Begin a satellite ministry away from the present location aimed at reaching a different segment of the population. Although there are many examples now of multiple-site congregations, here are two examples from small congregations. Both First UMC in Sedalia, Missouri, and St. Luke's Episcopal in Park City, Utah, developed two sites when they had a worship attendance of approximately two hundred.

- Attempt the "One-Two-Three Hour" parking experiment. Instead of the traditional parking method, where every car has its own free space to come and go, you provide a row for one-hour parking, two-hour parking, and three-hour parking. Attendants in the lot help people find the right row. Since the two- and three-hour cars can't be moved for that amount of time, have one free rental car on hand for anyone to take in an emergency.

For Stage Three and Four Congregations Needing to Expand

In my experience, an old established church begins to grow because of the efforts of a new, energetic, outgoing, transformational pastor. Usually the church has less than four acres and has reached the point where it is out of room for both parking and worship space. Sphere Three and Four congregations like this have at least the following options:

- Sell the property and relocate. This is a good option if the congregation is unable to reach the people in the area. Perhaps another group of Christians will be able to reach those in the area.

- Buy any adjacent land, no matter what the price. The danger with this option is that buying property and tearing down houses may antagonize the neighbors to the point that the congregation has too much bad press in the area.

- Stay where they are, purchase property in another section of the city, begin a satellite ministry, and become a church in two locations with the option of relocating in ten or more years. The number of Sphere Three and Four congregations developing multi-site ministries is steadily growing. Both Community Christian Church in Naperville, Illinois, (http://www.communitychristian.org) and First UMC in Houston, Texas, have been doing this for some time now and have a good-size congregation at both sites. First Baptist Church in Arlington, Texas, has so many locations it is almost impossible to count them all. Worship attendance at these numerous locations totals 3700, not counting the attendance at the mother church. For more examples of multi-site ministries see:
  http://www.easumbandy.com/FAQS/multiplesitechurches.htm.

- Give away one hundred people to plant a new congregation in the area, and begin rebuilding the mother congregation. I think the postmodern church will use this option more than Baby Boomer congregations. New Hope Christian Fellowship is one of the most aggressive congregations that has used this option in its first wave of church planting. However, they warn people not to send too many people because it can ruin the pioneer spirit of the planter. (http://www.newhope-hawaii.org/)

- Begin a third worship service during Sunday school and do one or more of the following: develop one-, two-, and three-hour parking lots; hire an off-duty police person to facilitate in and out traffic; develop a parking lot team of servants to help people find parking; shuttle the key leaders to and from a nearby parking lot that is unused on Sunday. The church where I served Christ for twenty-four years began such a service in 1975, and it became our largest service with the most unconnected people.

Innovative Options for New Congregations

More and more ministry is being attempted now without purchasing buildings. Some never intend to purchase land, and some are waiting much longer to do so. In addition to those options listed above in the section of "Space and Place as Metaphor," here are some additional examples:

- Saddleback Church in Lake Forest, California, had over fifty rented locations and over 5,000 in attendance before it purchased its present property.
(http://www.saddleback.org/home/welcome.asp)

- New Hope Christian Fellowship, which meets in a rented school auditorium, has grown to over 8,000 in worship in six years. (http://www.newhope-hawaii.org/)

- Hope Community Church Network in Seattle, Washington, is a cluster of new churches started by Doug Murren. The key is not the size of the congregation but penetration into the city of Seattle. (http://www.web-rock.com/hope)

- The house and cell church movements are alive and well and growing. (http://www.house2house.tv/,

http://www.outreach.ca/cpc/Housechurches.htm, and
http://www.touchusa.org/)

- Spirit Garage in Minneapolis, Minnesota, meets in the
  Minneapolis Theatre Garage. Here are the directions to the
  church from their website: "Theatre Garage is located on
  Franklin Avenue, at the southwest corner of Lyndale
  Avenue. It's a squat brick building with a sign facing
  Lyndale Avenue, right next to the Coffee Gallery and across
  the street diagonally from Rudolph's barbeque."
  (http://www.spiritgarage.org/)

- Frontline Church in Falls Church, Virginia, is one of the best
  examples of starting a church within an existing church to
  reach a new culture. (http://www.frontline.to/)

- The cyber church may well be one of the largest congrega-
  tions in the world in a few years. Some examples:
  Cyberchurch of the Remnant
  (http://www.hawaiian.net/~rnpilot/church.html);
  The Cyber Church (http://thecyberchurch.org/);
  First Church of Cyberspace (http://www.godweb.org/).

As more and more innovative congregations place mission above
space and place, many more new ways of overcoming the limitations of space or the lack of funds will be found. One thing is for
sure: these congregations are proving that, like the congregations of
the first century, what is important is not if you have a place of your
own, but how creatively you use the space you have.

Foundational Nuts and Bolts

As in any discipline, the effective use of property has a few givens.
Here is a list of the absolute essentials:

- Educational space never pays for itself. If you need both educational and worship space and plan to build, build the worship
  space first. Usually, if you can't get people into worship, you
  won't get them into educational experiences. Also, more and
  more educational opportunities are happening off campus.

- Mergers usually leave the merged congregation weaker in two years than before it merged—unless all present property is sold, new property purchased, and a new name is found that is not hyphenated.

- People need twenty-four inches to sit on.

- You can only use eighty percent of anything on an average day. If you are using averages to determine seating or parking capacity, keep in mind that every other Sunday is above the average and that on special days averages don't mean much.

- You can usually raise twenty-five to forty percent more for construction if you hire someone from the outside to do your capital fund drive.

- Avoid a yearly mortgage payment of more than twenty-eight percent of your annual budget or a total debt of no more than twice your budget.

- You need a minimum of one off-street parking space for every two people on the property at the peak hour.

- It's hard to raise money to pay off an existing debt.

- In traditional settings where a church owns its own property it takes about one acre for every hundred people in worship today.

- Organized congregations can have as little as ten minutes between worship services if they have adequate parking and flow in and out of the worship area.

- Additional facilities will not cause a church to grow, but they will hinder it from growing.

- Put off construction as long as possible. An example is Ginghamsburg UMC in Tipp City, Ohio. They grew to almost 1500 in a worship center that can handle around 250. They had back-to-back worship services at forty-five minute intervals with people hanging out the windows Troas style. As a result, they were able to gain a large critical mass before they built, allowing them to purchase a ninety-acre tract and build a multipurpose worship center. (http://www.ginghamsburg.org/).

- Don't allow aesthetics to hinder function. I've seen many beautiful buildings with great theological significance that are a functional nightmare.

The following statements will help you determine if you need focus on this unfreezing move.

❑ Where we are located now is exactly where we would locate if we were buying property today to begin the church.

❑ As you drive by our church, the facilities shout out to you "Come on in; we'll take good care of you."

❑ Our facilities have the latest technology.

❑ Our sound system allows people to hear the spoken word without straining and amplifies the music so it fills the room.

❑ We have an off-street parking space for every two people on the premises at the peak hour.

❑ Using twenty-four inches per person as our guide, our worship average is seldom more than eighty percent of the capacity.

❑ Our nursery is safe, dedicated just to children, on the same floor as the sanctuary, and is well staffed by the same paid servants from week to week.

❑ We have diaper-changing tables in both the women's and men's restrooms.

Our average score is:

1–2: Green Light   **3–4:** Yellow Light   **5 or above:** Red Light

---

1. Case in point is Southeast Christian Center in Louisville, Kentucky. Its attendance jumped from 9,000 to 13,000 (actually it was higher the Sunday they moved into their new $95 million dollar plant (http://southeastchristian.org/). In the same way, if a congregation is alive and feeding its people and runs out of room, the lack of facilities can stifle the growth. So facilities can make a difference when something good is going on inside.

Chapter 10
Money Is Your Least Concern

Money is the last unfreezing move because it seldom plays a large part in transformation or innovation. Far too many church leaders believe that all their problems would be solved if they could just balance the budget or find more money for a new project. Nothing could be further from the truth. The abundance or lack of money is usually directly related to the way a congregation approaches the first and fourth unfreezing moves. If you develop strong spiritual giants who are involved in mission, then money is seldom an issue. So this chapter will be short.

Unfreezing Move Nine: Radical Generosity

Luke 21:3–4

The vast majority of Sphere Three and Four congregations in the twenty-first century are changing the way leaders understand money issues in two ways. They define stewardship as a way of life rather than a method of raising money. Stewardship is based upon the belief that everything you have, including your life, is owned by God. You are merely a steward or trustee of it. Stewardship refers to how you use everything you have.

Sphere Three and Four congregations make accountability for what one has been given an essential part of one's discipleship process. Serious participants are taught by precept and example that money is merely one of the many things Christians must master. As a result, these congregations are abandoning the use of once-a-year, hard-sell, stewardship programs and drives. They understand that more and more people are growing up outside of the Christian culture and are less likely to see the need to support religious institutions, even when they attend them. The postmodern response to the stewardship of money is Why should I give? not What is the best way for me to give? Sphere Three and Four congregations address the why question rather than play on the person's guilt.

Sphere Three and Four congregations learn to rely on methods much closer to those of the first century. New Testament congregations were admonished by Paul to practice two kinds of giving: 1) systematic, first-day-of-the-week, generous giving to the care and feeding of Christians and the poor everywhere; and 2) second mile or designated giving to specific causes, usually helping needy congregations or supporting apostles. Sphere Three and Four congregations teach leaders to live out a form of radical generosity that goes far beyond how they give their money. Spiritual giants become radically generous people.

New Testament congregations used money in four ways: 1) to meet the financial needs of believers within the body, both local and non-local; 2) to meet the needs of the poor and widows (widows didn't have Social Security, Medicare and Medicaid); 3) to meet the financial needs of those unconnected to the church; and 4) to provide financial support for apostles (today's missionaries). Nothing is said about providing for the support of physical plants.

On the other hand, Sphere One and Two congregations spend fifty-five percent to ninety-five percent of their income on salaries and facilities. Many of these congregations count the year successful if they are able keep the roof repaired, the furnace burning, and the pastor paid. You know the old adage, "Show me a person's checkbook, and I'll tell you their priorities."

Guidelines for Radical Generosity

Many Sphere Three and Four congregations are now in the process of abandoning the annual fund-raising campaign in favor of a biblical model of radical generosity. The following guidelines can assist you in developing a biblical approach to finances:

- Focus everything on generous giving. Generous giving follows six things:
  1. A clear sense of mission: The more owned and managed the Mission, Vision, and Values of the congregation, the more generous the giver.

2. Trust between the congregation and the leaders: Continually work on the first unfreezing move and give full disclosure of all funds

3. Relevancy of the mission: Donors give to big dreams much more than to congregational needs.

4. Personal involvement in the mission to which the person is giving: If you are consistently working the fourth unfreezing move, you already know this.

5. A person's values: If the Gospel does not shape them, the giving level is likely to be low. Focus on disciple making rather than fund raising.

6. Leaders who are role models of stewardship of money: The pastor is the primary leader of giving and should inform the congregation how much he or she gives and why. Some consider this grandstanding. The real truth is that it is good role modeling. Pastors should not be afraid to talk about *their entire* spiritual journey.

- Don't be afraid to talk or preach about money as an essential part of stewardship. Jesus said more about money than any other one subject because he knew the human heart. No one reaches the spiritual depth to which they are capable without first mastering their money. Christian leaders who avoid talking about money do a disservice to the people they lead. When money is included in the stewardship of life, it is appropriate to talk about it anytime during the year.

- Make an explanation of generous giving and/or tithing a regular part of new participants' orientation

- Redefine the Stewardship Committee or team so that it is responsible for stewardship as defined above. I suggest doing away with the Stewardship Committee and making the stewardship of money part of the growth process in Lay Mobilization. Make stewardship of life a year-round emphasis with money being only one of many aspects. You might divide the year into four emphases: prayer, attendance, gifts, and service; and ask people to commit to being good stewards of each of these areas of their lives.

- Ask people to support a specific mission and give them several options during the year, but avoid asking for support of the institution or the denomination.

Suggestions for the Transition

- Don't abandon the annual finance campaign until you have grown your leaders into spiritual giants. This often takes two to four years.

- Don't let the Finance Committee get near the annual campaign because they typically put limits on the process.

- Choose only spiritual giants to lead the campaign. I'm referring to how much the person gives in relation to his or her capability, not how much he or she gives. If you have the widow who gave her mite in your congregation, ask her to lead this campaign. God honors that kind of radical generosity.

- Do your "stewardship of money" drive first, and then draw up a budget. Encourage people to give because they want to, rather than because the church needs money.

- Talk about "percentage giving" and tithing; never discuss giving one's "fair share." Ask people to begin stepping up toward a tithe. Each year stress how many people are beginning to tithe and move toward getting everyone to tithe rather emphasizing how much was raised. Provide a place on the pledge card for people to note if they're tithing.

- Giving begets giving. Do away with the unified budget approach and encourage "second mile" or designated giving. Contrary to popular thought, designated giving will not harm regular giving to the budget. Unified budgets merely limit the amount of giving that occurs during the year. Designated giving is a way to encourage first-wave, unchurched Boomers to learn the art of giving and to take a step toward the goal of tithing.

- Stop passing the offering plate during worship. Instead, place large offering boxes at the exits, and mail out offering envelopes to everyone each month. Often, leaders who give once a month, or entrepreneurs who are paid now and then, put a dollar in the plate as it's passed, so they have something to put in the plate. This provides a poor example for visitors and new Christians to see.

- In our time, people give out of three pockets: 1) systematic regular giving; 2) special appeals for designated missions; and 3) planned giving from one's estate. The one most often overlooked is planned giving. I call this to your attention because over the next few years trillions of dollars will change hands due to the transfer of wealth from one generation to the next. Caution: Do not allow endowments to be restricted solely for the maintenance of the facilities. Instead encourage endowments to be given to a variety of things such as starting new ministries, adding staff to begin a new ministry, planting congregations, and supporting missionaries. Never use your endowments for operational expenses. It may keep the institutional church alive, but it seldom develops stewards who understand radical generosity.

Now That You Are Past the Transition

Once you have made the transition from annual campaigns to a more biblical form of giving, consider incorporating the following:

- Either include radical generosity in the requirements for leadership or for membership. Remember, discipleship rather than membership is your goal, so don't worry about raising the bar of membership. The higher you raise it, the more spiritual giants you will deliver.

- Encourage either tithing—or something beyond tithing—as the goal of radical generosity.

- Never allow anyone to assume a key leadership role who is not an example of radical generosity.

- Pay for building projects as you go rather than borrowing the money.

A Quick Word About Tithing

I personally believe in tithing, not because the Scriptures demand it, but because it gives me a time-honored measuring rod. However, I don't see tithing as a goal that limits the amount one gives. The goal of radical generosity is for people to reach the point where their standard of giving determines their standard of living rather than their standard of living determining their standard of giving. For those who make millions, tithing is a hindrance, since giving ten percent does little to determine their standard of living. However, giving fifty or sixty percent might determine a millionaire's standard of living.

I prefer the wisdom of John Wesley. He said, "Earn all you can. Save all you can. Give all you can."[1] Such advice develops stewards, and if you develop stewards instead of church members, the finances will fall into place.

> **One's standard of giving should determine one's standard of living rather than one's standard of living determining one's standard of giving.**

The following statements will assist you in determining if you should focus on this unfreezing move.

❏ We focus on year-round stewardship of life.

❏ We do not have an annual stewardship of money drive.

❏ Our key leaders are expected to at least tithe.

❏ Our annual giving exceeds four percent of the average household income in our area.

❏ Stewardship of life, including money, is an essential part of our participants' orientation.

❏ Our leaders, and especially our pastor, are not afraid to talk about money.

❏ Our pastor tells us each year how much he or she is giving.

Our average score is:

1–2: Green Light   **3–4:** Yellow Light   **5 or above:** Red Light

Endnotes

1. John Wesley, *Selected Letters of John Wesley*, ed. Frederick C. Gill (New York: Philosophical Library, 1956), p. 175.

Epilogue
Are You Ready to Join Jesus on the Mission Field?

By now you should have some idea of where you need to begin your movement toward permission-giving and innovation. So a question begs to be asked and answered: Are you ready to join Jesus on the mission field?

If this question makes you feel like Peter, whom Jesus beckoned to step out of the boat and come to him, remember that the first step is always the hardest. It takes a great deal of faith for leaders in Sphere One or Two congregations to take the first step toward becoming an effective congregation. It also takes a lot of courage for leaders in Sphere Three and Four congregations, where everything is humming along, to fix something before it's broken. And it takes a quantum step of faith to personally join Jesus on the mission field.

So…where is Jesus' mission field? Wherever you are—your living room, driveway, backyard, place of business, attending a sporting event or other recreational activity, or surfing online. You may even find an opportunity to share with the person sitting in the pew next to you or in that dull committee meeting. The mission field is anywhere you find people on a spiritual journey. Once you're out in the mission field, the key to connecting with the unconnected is simple: when they open the door for spiritual conversation, share your story with them. Share with them what it is about your relationship with Jesus that you find so essential for your life. It's that simple. But first you have to join Jesus on the mission field long enough to form solid relationships with people with whom you have a natural affinity.

If you still need more pointing toward the mission field, visit this section of our website:

http://www.easumbandy.com/FAQS/connectwithunchurched.htm.

The Beginning

It is my prayer that this book has given you assistance in determining what action to take to achieve God's dream for your congregation. Don't expect overnight miracles. It has taken decades for Sphere One and Two congregations to become what they are today. You will not lead your church into becoming a Sphere Three congregation overnight. Similarly, it takes time for Sphere Three and Four congregations to become constantly innovative.

So here is my best advice for congregations in all four spheres of life. Pray and work hard on the unfreezing move that you feel is the place to focus; and remember, if you don't have the leaders to pull it off, pray and wait for God to send what you need your way. The two disciples walking along the road to Emmaus didn't have what they needed for the journey until they lingered awhile with Jesus. Staying in touch with your relationship with Jesus is essential for joining him on the mission field.

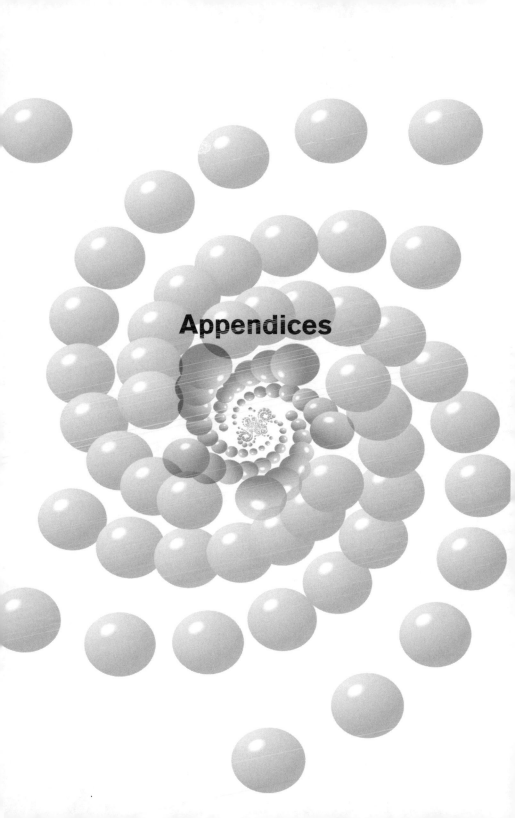

Appendices

Appendix A

Permission-Giving Inventory[1]

Answer the following questions with 1 being an unqualified Yes and 10 being an unqualified No.

1. Our church leaders believe that people doing the actual ministry should make the majority of the decisions that affect how they do their ministry.

   1   2   3   4   5   6   7   8   9   10

2. People at the lowest level of organization in our church should be able to suggest and implement improvements to their own ministry without going through several committees and levels of approval.

   1   2   3   4   5   6   7   8   9   10

3. Each person in the congregation should be free to live out her or his spiritual gifts in the congregation without getting approval—even if it means starting a new ministry.

   1   2   3   4   5   6   7   8   9   10

4. The nature of our ministry lends itself to a team-based approach rather than to individual effort.

   1   2   3   4   5   6   7   8   9   10

5. Our leadership is flexible enough to permit restructuring or reorganization so that the organization facilitates the new mission of the church.

   1   2   3   4   5   6   7   8   9   10

6. It is possible to organize ministry so that teams can take responsibility for entire ministries.

1   2   3   4   5   6   7   8   9   10

7. There is enough complexity in our ministry to allow for initiative and decision-making.

1   2   3   4   5   6   7   8   9   10

8. Our leadership is comfortable with individuals or teams making autonomous, on the spot decisions.

1   2   3   4   5   6   7   8   9   10

9. The laity are interested in or willing to organize into teams or small groups.

1   2   3   4   5   6   7   8   9   10

10. Our key leadership is willing to share its power with those who are not in leadership.

1   2   3   4   5   6   7   8   9   10

11. Our church has a history of following through on new ideas.

1   2   3   4   5   6   7   8   9   10

12. Our key lay leadership is willing to radically change its own roles and behavior.

1   2   3   4   5   6   7   8   9   10

13. Our church is secure enough to guarantee a period of relative stability during which permission-giving can develop.

1   2   3   4   5   6   7   8   9   10

14. We have adequate resources to support and train our people.

1   2   3   4   5   6   7   8   9   10

15. Our staff and key lay leadership understands that becoming a permission-giving church is a lengthy, time-consuming, and labor-intensive process that may take five years and is willing to make the investment in time.

1   2   3   4   5   6   7   8   9   10

16. Our church has a network that could provide information to any lay person anytime.

1   2   3   4   5   6   7   8   9   10

17. Our lay people have the skills needed to take greater responsibility for the ministries of the church.

1   2   3   4   5   6   7   8   9   10

18. Our senior pastor is willing to invest in training team leaders.

1   2   3   4   5   6   7   8   9   10

19. Our Finance and Trustee Committees exist to serve the needs of those trying to implement ministry.

1   2   3   4   5   6   7   8   9   10

20. Our leaders are more concerned with discovering ways to reach the unchurched than with how those ministries are discovered or implemented.

1   2   3   4   5   6   7   8   9   10

If your total score is under 60, you or your group is ready for permission-giving, team-based ministry. If the score is between 60–70, there is work to be done on the high score questions, but the church may begin the transition. If the average scores are over 80, forget permission giving for now and begin major remedial work.

1 This inventory appeared originally in my book *Sacred Cows Make Gourmet Burgers* (Nashille: Abingdon, 1995).

Appendix B

Resources

Because authentic mission stems from the passions of individuals not institutions, and because we are living in a time when the issues and challenges congregations face are changing much faster than ever before, it is impossible to give a cookie cutter list of the best ministries or programs available to congregations that want to be effective Sphere Three and Four congregations in the twenty-first century. I can mention some of the present ministries that are transforming individuals, congregations, and communities. You must keep in mind that there is no guarantee that any of these will work in your congregation or if it does, that it will continue to be effective for much longer. You must also realize that these resources represent a wide range of theological perspectives.

The resources are divided into four sections: Books, Workbooks/-Manuals, Websites, and Organizations. Have fun with them.

Introduction: What This Book Is About

Books

- Guder, Darrell L., *The Continuing Conversion of the Church* (Grand Rapids: Eerdmans, 2000) and *Missional Church: A Vision for the Sending of the Church in North America* (Grand Rapids: Eerdmans, 1998).

- Miller, Donald, *Reinventing American Protestantism: Christianity in the New Millennium* (Berkley: University of California, 1997).

- McGavran, Donald, *The Bridges of God: A Study in the Strategy of Missions* (Fuller Seminary Bookstore, Reprint 1996).

- Van Gelder, Craig, *The Essence of the Church* (Grand Rapids: Baker Books, 2000).

Chapter One: Christianity Is an Organic Movement

Books

- Caird, G. B., *The Apostolic Age* (London: Duckworth, 1955).

- Comby, Jean, *How to Read Church History* (New York: Crossroads, 1985).

- Easum, Bill, *Leadership on the OtherSide* (Nashville: Abingdon, 2000).

- Elwell, Walter A. and Yarbrough, Robert W., eds., *Readings From the First-Century World* (Grand Rapids: Baker, 1998).

- Gibbs, Eddie, *Church Next: Quantum Changes in How We Do Ministry* (Downers Grove: InterVarsity Press, 2000).

- Latourette, Kenneth Scott, *A History of Christianity, Vol. 1: Beginnings to 1500* (San Francisco: Harper, 1975).

Chapter Two: The Systems Story

Books

- Bandy, Thomas G., *Kicking Habits: Welcome Relief for Addicted Churches* upgrade (Nashville: Abingdon Press, 2001).

- Beck, Nuala, *Shifting Gears* (Toronto: Harper, 1992).

- Senge, Peter, *The Fifth Discipline Fieldbook* (New York: Currency, 1994).

Chapter Three: Permission-Giving Communities Of Faith

Books

- Ashkenas, Ron, *The Boundaryless Organization: Breaking Down the Chains of Organizational Structure* (San Francisco: Jossey-Bass, 1998).

- Easum, William M, *Sacred Cows Make Gourmet Burgers* (Nashville: Abingdon, 1995)

Websites

- Easum, William M., *"Nine Texts For Our Time"* (http://www.easumbandy.com/netresul/Easum/01–05.htm)

- For a list of permission-giving congregations in 1998 see http://www.easumbandy.com/FAQS/permissiongivingchurches.htm

Chapter Four: The Innovative Congregation

Books

- Bandy, Thomas G., *Moving off the Map* (Nashville: Abingdon Press, 1998) and *Christian Chaos* (Nashville: Abingdon Press, 1999).

- Collins, James C. and Porra, Jerry I., *Built to Last* (San Francisco: Harper Business, 1997).

- Rogers, Everett R., *Diffusion of Innovations* (New York: Free Press, 1995).

- Schaller, Lyle, *Discontinuity and Hope: Radical Change and the Path to the Future* (Nashville: Abingdon Press, 1999).

Chapter Five: The Foundations of Transformation and Innovation

Books

- Payne, Claude and Beazley, Hamilton, *Reclaiming the Great Commission: A Practical Model for Transforming Denominations and Congregations* (San Francisco: Jossey-Bass, 2000).

Websites

- For more information on Lewin's work on unfreezing moves see: http://www.solonline.org/res/wp/10006.html and http://www.managementfirst.com/professional_organisations/information_management.htm

Chapter Six: The Two Foundational Unfreezing Moves

Unfreezing Move One: A Solid Community of Faith

Spiritual Leadership

Books

- Bandy, Thomas G., *Coaching Change* (Nashville: Abingdon Press, 2000).

- Bardwick, Judith, *Danger In The Comfort Zone* (New York: American Management Association, 1993).

- Barry, William A., *The Practice of Spiritual Direction* (San Francisco: Harper, 1986).

- Burns, James, *Leadership* (San Francisco: Harper Collins, 1985).

- Carver, John and Miriam, *Reinventing Your Board* (San Francisco: Jossey-Bass, 1997).

- Easum, Bill, *Leadership on the OtherSide* (Nashville: Abingdon Press, 2000).

- Easum, William M., *The Church Growth Handbook* (Nashville: Abingdon Press, 1990).

- Foster, Richard, *Celebration of Discipline: The Path to Spiritual Growth* (San Francisco: Harper, 1988).

- Heifetz, Ronald H., *Leadership Without Easy Answers* (Cambridge: Belknap Press, 1994).

- Kelsey, Morton T., *Companions on the Inner Way: The Art of Spiritual Guidance* (Crossroad Publishing Co 1995).

- Merton, Thomas, *Spiritual Direction & Meditation* (Collegeville, MN: The Liturgical Press, 1960).

- Mottola, Anthony, trns. *The Spiritual Exercises of St. Ignatius* (New York: Image Books, 1964).

162

- Rogers, Everett M., *Diffusion of Innovations* (New York: The Free Press, 1995).

- Townsend, Patrick L., Gebhardt, Joan E., and Austin, Nancy K., *Five Star Leadership* (New York: John Wiley, 1999).

- Wheatley, Margaret, *Leadership and the New Science* (San Francisco: Jossey-Bass, 1999).

- Wills, Dick, *Waking to God's Dream* (Nashville: Abingdon Press, 1999).

Workbooks/Manuals

- Disciple Bible Study is a United Methodist publication but is suitable for any mainline denomination. It includes videos, but requires training first (36 weeks). Contact UMPH at 800-672-1789 at P.O. Box 801, Nashville, TN 37202 or go to http://www.umph.com/.

- *Vital Christianity: A Manual for Teaching the Basics of Christianity.* This is basic curriculum for any level of Christian. Available from Ginghamsburg United Methodist Church, Tipp City, Ohio. 513-667-1069 (www.ginghamsburg.org).

- "The Marks of a Disciple" from Prince of Peace Lutheran Church and "Changing Church" (www.changingchurch.org).

- "Contagious Christians," available from Zondervan, 1-800-727-3480, (www.willowcreek.org).

- "Experiencing God" (13 weeks) Mike Rogers and Claude V. King, Kingdom Agenda Ministries, 1395 Michigan Blvd., Dunedin, FL 34698.

- "Mind of Christ" (18 weeks) is a followup to Henry Blackaby's *Experiencing God* (Nashville: Lifeway, 1998). (http://www.lifeway.com/)

Websites

- For one-on-one coaching with Bill Easum contact (mailto:Easum@easumbandy.com).

Organizations

- Emmaus (Emmaus Journey, 6960 Snowbird Drive, Colorado Springs, CO 80918), Telephone: 719-599-0448 (mailto:info@emmausjourney.org).

- Shalem Institute for Spiritual Formation, 5430 Grosvenor Lane, Bethesda, MD 20814. Telephone: 301-897-7334. They have a school for spiritual directors.

Functions Around Trust

Books

Shaw, Robert Bruce, *Trust in the Balance*, (San Francisco: Jossey Bass, 1997).

Conflict

Books

- Haugk, Kenneth C., *Antagonists in the Church* (Minneapolis: Augsburg, 1988)

- Pritchett & Associates, *Resistance: Moving Beyond the Barriers to Change* (Pritchett & Associates, 1996).

- Rediger, G. Lloyd, *Clergy Killers* (Lousville: Westminster Press, 1997).

- Susek, Ron, *Firestorm* (Grand Rapids: Baker Book House, 1999).

Workbooks/Manuals

- Patton, Jeff. *Resolving Conflict* (EBA essential book: www.easumbandy.com)

Websites

- The FAQS section of our website has a section on Conflict Management. See http://www.easumbandy.com/FAQS/index.htm

- For more see http://www.easumbandy.com/FAQS/conflict_management.html

Organizations

- Alban Institute has several excellent pieces by Speed Leas. http://www.alban.org.

- Easum Bandy & Associates has two skilled consultants in conflict resolution.

- L.E.A.D. Consultants: Contact John Savage, Box 664, Reynoldsburg, OH 43068. Telephone: 614-864–0156 (www.leadinc.com).

A Desire to Connect With the Outside World

Books

- *Groups Investigating God*, "GIG" 2100 Productions, 608-274-9001.

- Richardson, Rick, *Evangelism Out of the Box*, (Downers Grove: InterVarsity Press, 2000).

Websites

- Servant Evangelism: See (www.kindness.com).

Workbooks/Manuals

- Alpha (15 weeks), level one: For a brief description of this program and how to reach Alpha, go to the FAQ's section of our website at http://www.easumbandy.com/FAQS/index.htm. Alpha is a new member study course that takes people into the basics of faith. It centers on Jesus, not denominationalism. Contact Cook Communications Ministries, 4050 Lee Vance View, Colorado Springs, CO, 80918, 1-888-949-2574.

Unfreezing Move Two: Discovering and Articulating the DNA

Books

- Bandy, Thomas G., *Moving Off the Map* (Nashville: Abingdon Press, 1998).

- Blanchard, Ken, *Managing by Values* (San Francisco: Barrett-Koehler, 1997).

- Easum, Bill, *Leadership on the OtherSide* (Nashville: Abingdon Press, 2000).

- Jones, Laurie Beth, *The Path* (New York: Hyperion, 1998).

Workbooks/Manuals

- "Vision Discernment" by Thomas G. Bandy. Available at (www.easumbandy.com).

Websites

- See the FAQS section on our website: http://www.easumbandy.com/FAQS/mission_statements.htm.

Chapter Seven: An Inviting Growing and Sending Community of Faith

Unfreezing Move Three: Indigenous Worship

Books

- Arn, Charles, *How to Start a New Service* (Grand Rapids: Baker Book House, 1997).

- Easum, William M. and Bandy, Thomas G., *Growing Spiritual Redwoods* (Nashville: Abingdon Press, 1998).

- Morgenthaler, Sally, *Worship Evangelism* (Grand Rapids: Zondervan, 1995).

- Sample, Tex, *The Spectacle of Worship in a Wired World* (Nashville: Abingdon Press, 1998).

- Slaughter, Michael, *Out on the Edge* (Nashville: Abingdon Press, 1998).

- Wilson, Len, *The Wired Church* (Nashville: Abingdon Press, 1999).

Workbooks/Manuals

- "Worship for People of the Heart," by Bill Easum. Available at (www.easumbandy.com).

- "The Power of Teams," Video from Ginghamsburg UMC (www.ginghamsburg.org).

Websites

- See the FAQ's section of our website for a long list of worship helps. http://www.easumbandy.com/FAQS/index.htm.

- Jason Moore and Len Wilson of Lumicon provide worship graphics (http://www.lumicon.org).

Unfreezing Move Four:
Mobilizing the Congregation for Ministry

Books

- Arn, Charles and Win, *The Master's Plan for Making Disciples* (Grand Rapids: Baker Book House, 1998).

- Bright, Bill, *Witnessing Without Fear* (Nashville: Thomas Nelson, 1993).

- Cordeiro, Wayne, *Doing Church as a Team* (Ventura: Regal, 2001).

- Hybels, Bill, *Becoming a Contagious Christian* (Grand Rapids: Zondervan, 1996).

- Mallory, Sue, *The Equipping Church Guide* (Grand Rapids: Zondervan, 2001).

- Morris, Danny, *Yearning to Know God's Will* (Grand Rapids: Zondervan, 1992).

- Ogden, Greg, *The New Reformation*, (Grand Rapids: Zondervan, 1990).

- Steinborn, Melvin J., *The Lay Driven Church* (Ventura: Regal, 1992).

- Warren, Rick, *The Purpose Driven Church* (Grand Rapids: Zondervan, 1995).

Workbooks/Manuals

- You can see the entire Fractalling Exercise on "Leadership on the OtherSide Study Guide CD," and the print version of *Leadership on the OtherSide Study Guide* has a detailed explanation. Both from EBA, http://www.easumbandy.com or call 361-749-5364.

- Blackaby, Henry T. and King, Claude V., *Experiencing God* (Nashville: Broadman & Holman, 1998).

Websites

- Go to http://www.easumbandy.com and click Free Resources, then Recommended Resources, then Laity.

- See the FAQ's section of our website for subjects such as Lay Pastors, Lay Ministries, and Permission Giving. http://www.easumbandy.com/FAQS/index.htm.

- See www.ltn.org.

Unfreezing Move Five: Redemptive Missional Opportunities

Books

- Dennison, Jack, *City Reaching: on the Road to Community Transformation* (Pasadena: William Carey, 1999).

Websites

- Alpha: See above.

- Servant Evangelism: See above.

- Sidewalk Sunday School: http://www.metroministries.com/Ministries/sidewalk_sunday_school.htm

- City Reaching: http://www.easumbandy.com/FAQS/city_reach.htm

- Mission Houston: http://www.missionhouston.org.
- House and Cell churches:
  www.outreach.ca/cpc/Housechurches.htm,
  http://www.touchusa.org.
- An assorted list of possibilities can be found at:
  http://www.easumbandy.com/FAQS/connectwithunchurched.htm.

Organizations

- Mid-week Christian schools and clubs such as: Logos, 1405
  Frey Road, Pittsburgh, PA 15235; Kids clubs, contact Heather
  Olson Bunnell at 219-672-3031; and Pioneer Clubs, Box 788,
  Wheaton, IL 60189–0788, Phone 708-293-1600
  (http://www.pioneerclubs.org).

Unfreezing Move Six: Organizing Around the DNA

Books

- Bandy, Thomas G., *Christian Chaos* (Nashville: Abingdon, 1999).
- Easum, William M., *How to Reach Baby Boomers* (Nashville: Abingdon, 1991).
- Easum, William M., *Sacred Cows Make Gourmet Burgers* (Nashville: Abindgon, 1995).
- Morgan, Gareth, *Images of Organization* (San Francisco: Jossey Bass, 1998).
- Pinchot, G.E., *The End of Bureaucracy and the Rise of the Intelligent Organization* (San Francisco: Barrett-Koehler, 1993).

Chapter Eight: Staffing for the Mission Field

Unfreezing Move Seven: Hire Servants, Not Professionals

Books

- Bickers, Dennis, *The Tentmaking Pastor: The Joy of Bivocational Ministry* (Grand Rapids: Baker Books, 2000).

- Schaller, Lyle, *Multiple Staff and the Large Church* (Nashville: Abingdon, 1980).

Workbooks/Manuals

- "Developing a Multiple Staff: Administration and Restructuring," (Revised September 1998, Easum, Bandy, & Associates).

- "Clergy/Staff Selection Tips," traditional approach, reprint articles, $12.00 from Net Results, 806-762-8094.

- Myers-Briggs Inventory: (http://mijuno.larc.nasa.gov/dfc/mb.html) and (http://www.advisorteam.com/user/ktsintro.asp).

- DISC: NAMS, 800-441–6267.

- Role Preference Inventory, 800-443-1976.

- Bugbee, Bruce and Cousins, Don, *Networking*, (Grand Rapids: Zondervan, 1994).

Websites

- For information about staffing salaries in the U.S., see Christianity Today, Inc. (http://www.christianityonline.com); The National Association of Church Business Administrators (http://www.nacbanet.org); and Leadership Network for churches of 1,000 or more in worship (http://www.leadnet.org).

- For job placement opportunities online, see http://pastorstaff.topcities.com.

- For a wide variety of staff issues especially for the pastor see www.pastors.com.

- See the FAQ's at our website, http://www.easumbandy.com/FAQS/index.htm.

Organizations

- Gallup has a great tool for evaluating prospective staff members. Ask for Rosanne Liesveld, 301 S. 68th St. Pl. Lincoln, NE 68510, 402-489-9000 (http://education.gallup.com).

- "Leadership Self Evaluation," reprint articles from Net Results, $12.00, 806-762-8094.

- Birkman International can help you in the selection of staff and key laity to give leadership to important positions. They are a worldwide, management consulting firm that is now interested in helping churches select and train leadership. 3040 Post Oak Blvd., Suite 1425, Houston, Texas 77056, 713-623-2760 (http://www.birkman.com).

- Willow Creek provides a page in its Willow Creek Association newsletter for churches looking for additional staff. Call 708-765-0070.

Chapter Nine: Getting the Most Out of Your Property

Unfreezing Move Eight: Place and Space as Metaphor

Books

- Bowman, Ray, and Hall, Eddy, *When Not to Build* (Grand Rapids: Baker Book House, 2000).

- Easum, William, *The Complete Ministry Audit* (Nashville: Abingdon Press, 1996) and "Growth Principle Thirteen." (See www.easumbandy.com.)

- Hanna, Jeff, Safe and Secure: The Alban Guide to Protecting Your Congregation (Bethesda: Alban Institute, 1999). (See www.alban.org).

- See the Nursery section in William M. Easum, *The Complete Ministry Audit* (Nashville: Abingdon Press, 1996).

Workbooks/Manuals

- "Church Facilities": for reprint articles ($12.00), contact Net Results at 806-762-8094.

Websites

- See http://easumbandy.com/FAQS/index.htm for several resources under Architect, Audio Consultants, Church Security, Facilities, Improvements, Renting Space, Sound Systems, Office Space, and Strip Malls.

- For help with sound see The Church Sound Network at http://www.jdbsound.com; Technologies for Worship Ministries at http://www.tfwm.com; and http://www.easumbandy.com/FAQS/sound_systems.htm.

Chapter Ten: Money Is Your Least Concern

Unfreezing Move Nine: Radical Generosity

Books

- Callahan, Kennon, *Effective Church Finances* (San Francisco: Harper, 1997).

Workbooks/Manuals

- See the FAQS section of our website for Bonds or Loans, Budgeting Around The Mission Statement, Finances, Grant Proposals, Money, Offering Plates, and Stewardship and Tithing.

- "The Missing Piece" (Stewardship workbook, 1995) by Bill Easum (http://www.easumbandy.com).

- "Consecration Sunday," by Herb Miller at (http://netresults.org).

- Schmidt, J. David, *Choosing to Live: Financing the Future of Religious Body Headquarters* (Milwaukee: Christian Stewardship Association, 1996).

Websites

- For information on how permission-giving congregations handle their finances, see http://www.easumbandy.com/FAQS/money.htm#churchbudget.

- Crown Ministries (http://www.crown.org).

Organizations

- The Horizons Company, LLC does capital funds and endowment campaigns. See http://www.easumbandy.com/horizons/index.htm.

Epilogue: Are You Ready to Join Jesus on the Mission Field?

Books

- Careaga, Andrew, *eMinistry: Connecting With the Net Generation* (Grand Rapids: Kregel, 2001).

- Crandall, Ron, *Witness* (a set with manual, journal, and video) (Nashville: Disciple Resources, 2001).

- Hohstadt, Thomas, *Dying to Live* (Nashville: Abingdon, 2002), eBook formats.

- Hunter, George G., *The Celtic Way Of Evangelism* (Nashville: Abingdon Press, 2000).

- McLaren, Brian, *A New Kind of Christian* (San Francisco: Jossey-Bass, 2000).

- Sjogren, Steve, *101 Ways To Reach Your Community* (Colorado Springs: NavPress, 2001).

- Slaughter, Michael, *Real Followers: Beyond Virtual Christianity* (Nashville: Abingdon Press, 1999).

- Wright, Timothy, *The Prodigal Hugging Church* (Minneapolis: Augsburg Fortress, 2001).

Websites

- http://www.easumbandy.com/FAQS/connectwithunchurched.htm
- http://www.kindness.com